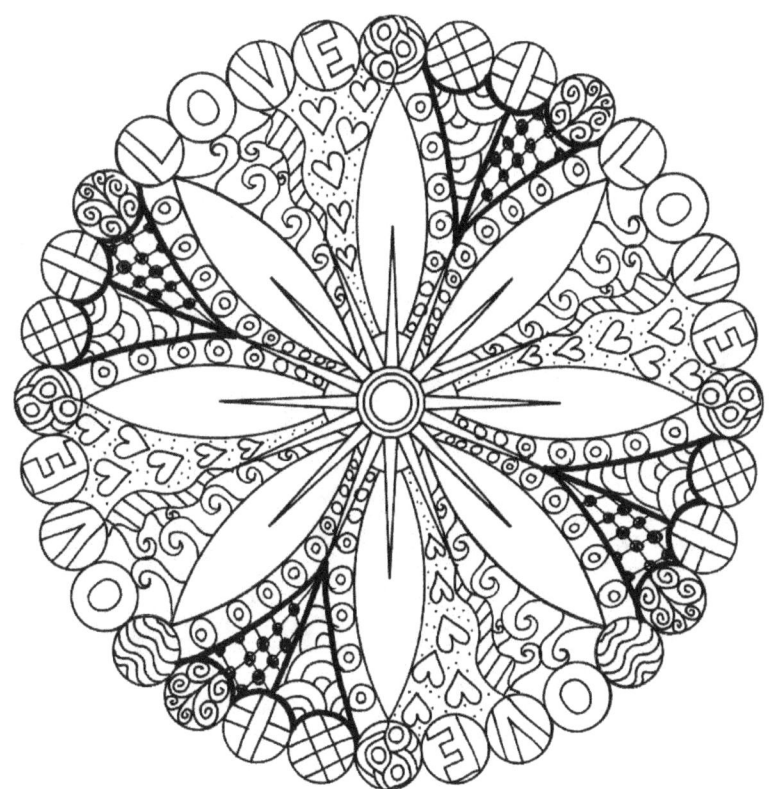

Fun & Fanciful Mandalas

For Adult Coloring Fun

Created by Kim A. Flodin

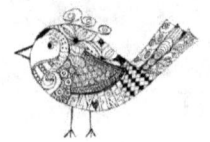

Fun & Fanciful Mandalas – First Edition

Copyright © 2015 Kim A. Flodin

ISBN-13: 978-1519462527

ISBN-10: 1519462522

Fun & Fanciful Mandalas are my versions of the mandala. I think mandalas are beautiful and amazing, but I've never really enjoyed coloring them…too stiff, too perfect somehow for my taste. So when I found a way to make an outline of a mandala and fill it with my own flowy art, now that was exciting! And, super fun to create and more importantly, color!
I hope you enjoy coloring them as much as I enjoyed creating and coloring them. ☺

As an intuitive energy healer, I put a little bit of what I call "magic" or you might call good vibes in every bit of art I create…it's my wish that you "feel" the vibe and have a great time coloring these whimsical and unique mandala designs.

Please share your Fun & Fanciful Mandalas with me on social media (tagged with my name- Kim Flodin) and I'll display them on my website and Instagram, Facebook, Twitter, etc.

Follow me and find me on the internet and social media by searching for
Keleki Love

I can't wait to see your Fun & Fanciful Mandalas!

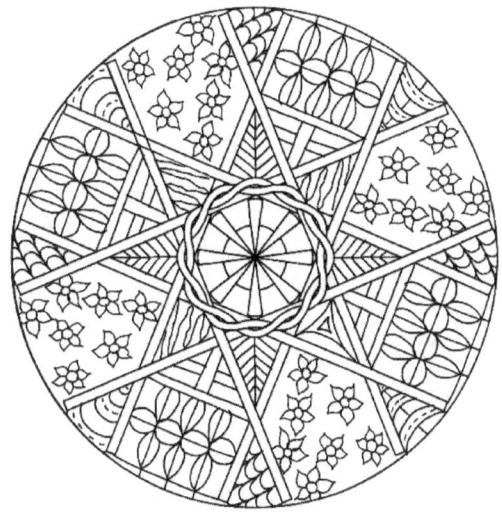

Please note: All of these mandala designs are hand drawn and therefore you may notice occasional irregularities, which naturally occur in hand-drawn art.

Visit my website http://kelekilove.wix.com/kelekilove to see more art and ideas for coloring.

If you enjoy this book, please leave me a review on Amazon.com.
I am an independent artist who is following her bliss with the goal of becoming an independent and abundant artist and appreciate your feedback and support.

If you would like to learn more about my goal to become an abundant artist, please visit my Patreon page: https://www.patreon.com/KelekiLove

I also have other books available for your coloring enjoyment.
Search for Kim A. Flodin on Amazon.

If you are interested in any of my healing services
or have feedback or comments to share with me directly,
please feel free to contact me at Keleki.love@yahoo.com

THANK YOU

Thank you to everyone who has supported me in my quest as an artist. So many people have encouraged me, shared my work and cheered me on. Thank you for your support. You have no idea how much it has meant to me! ☺

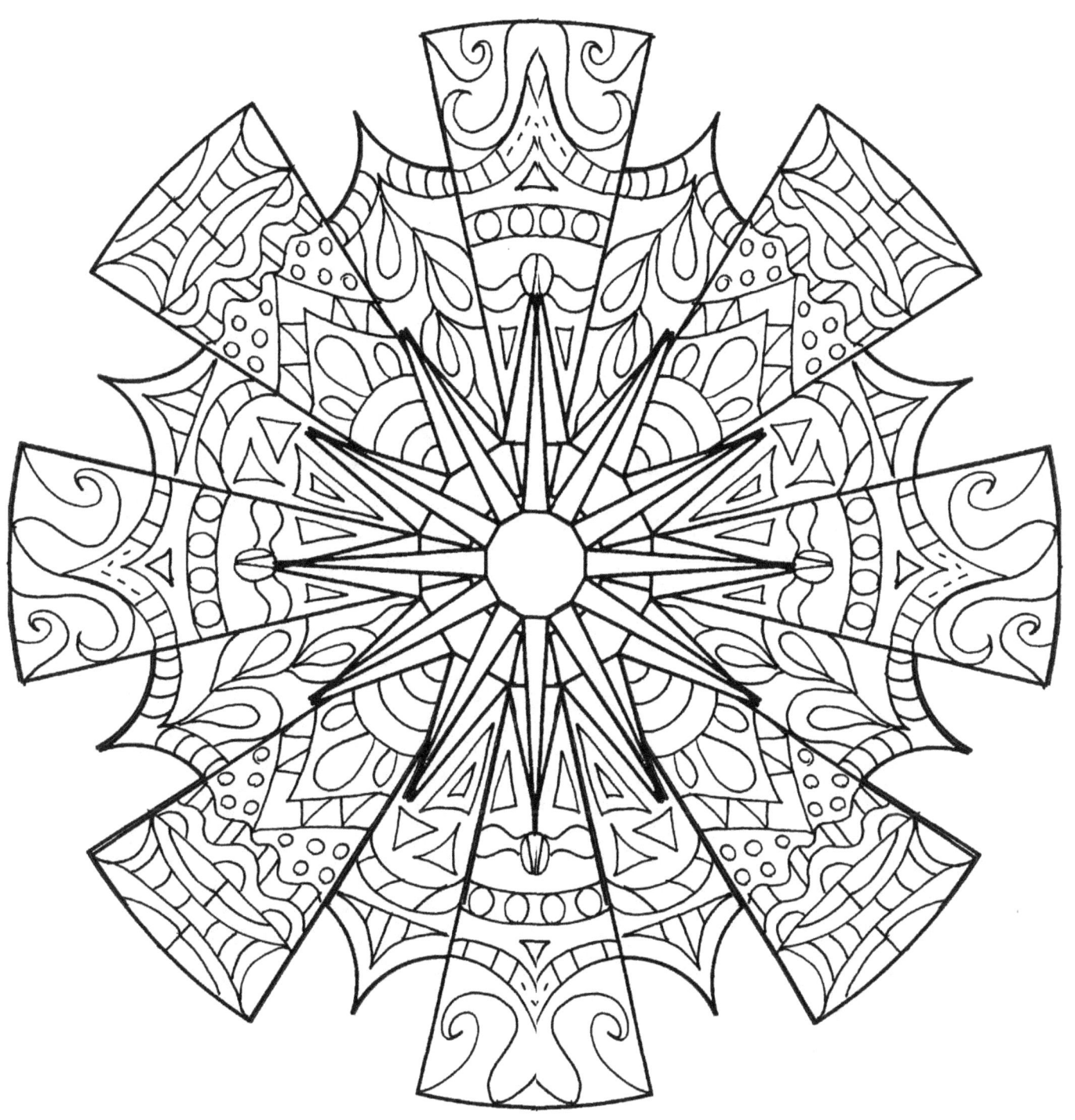

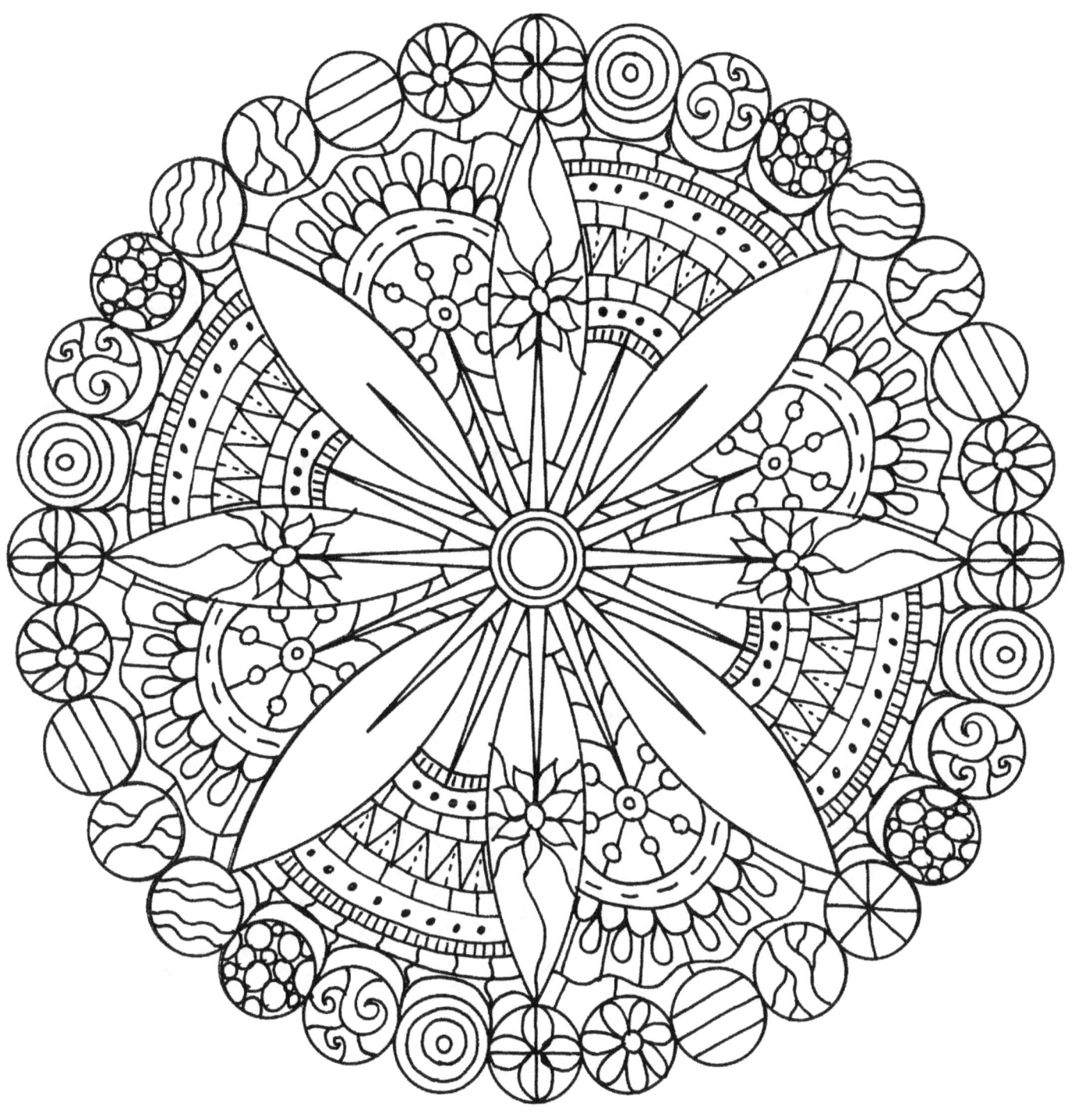

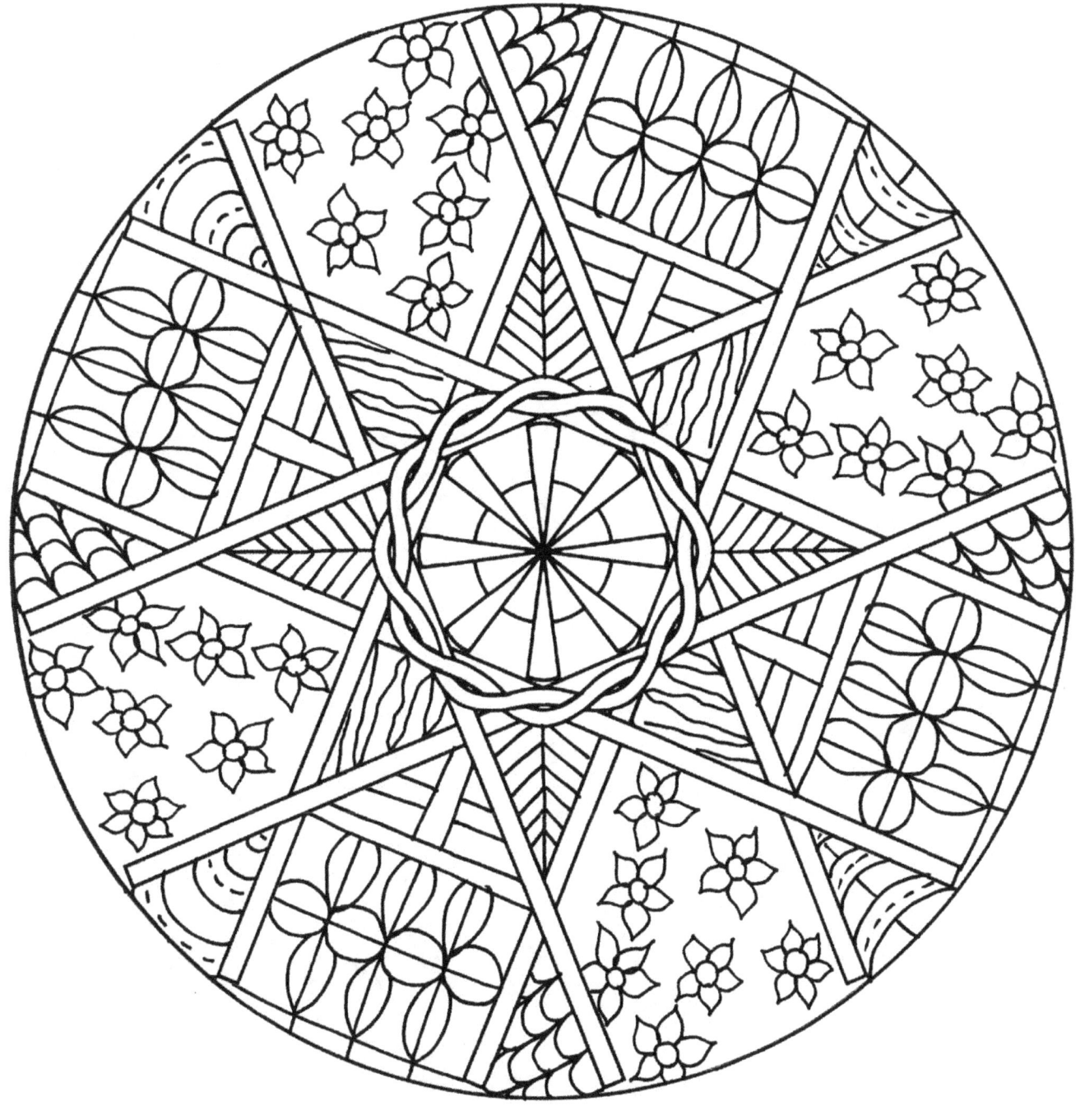

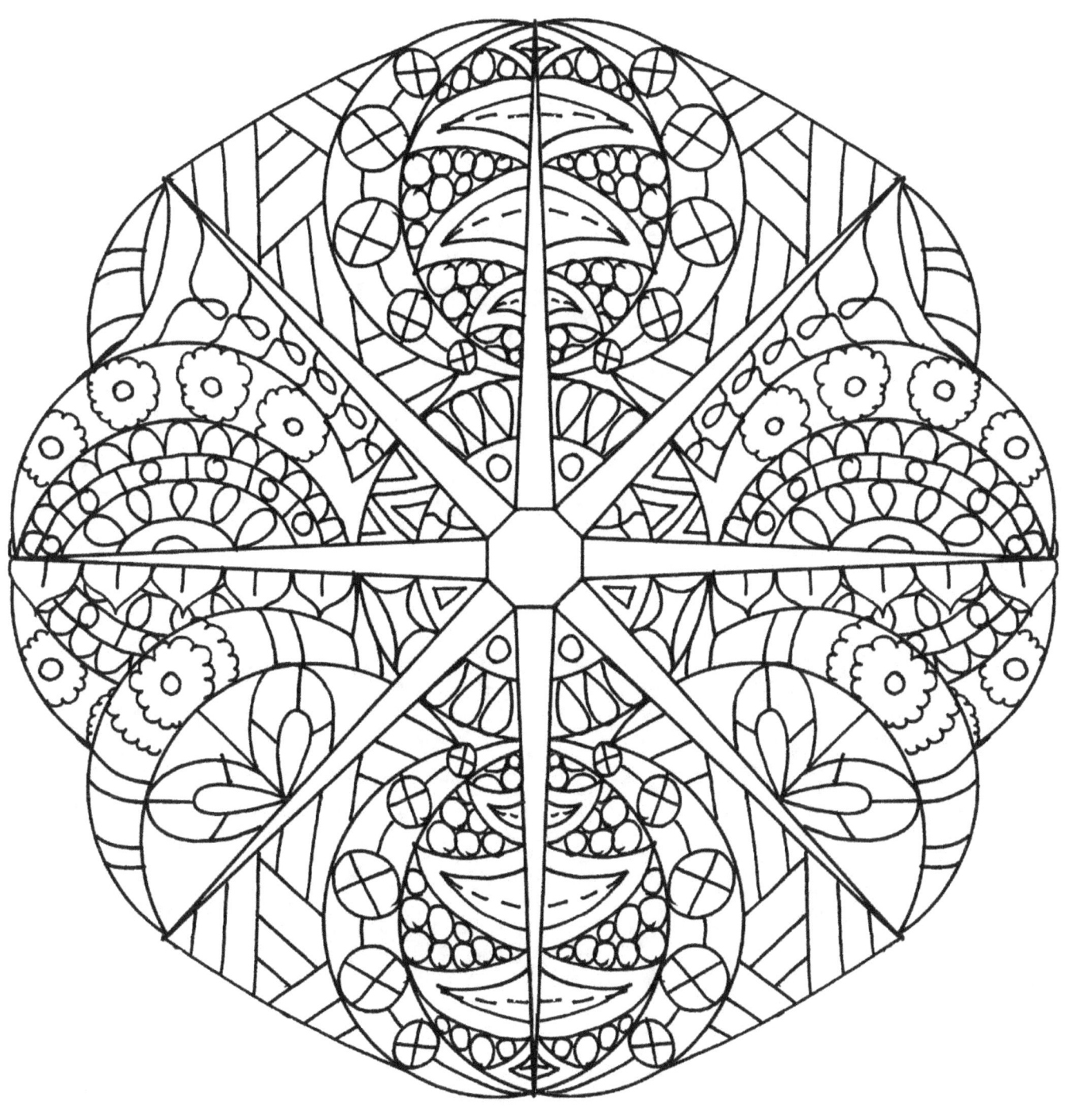

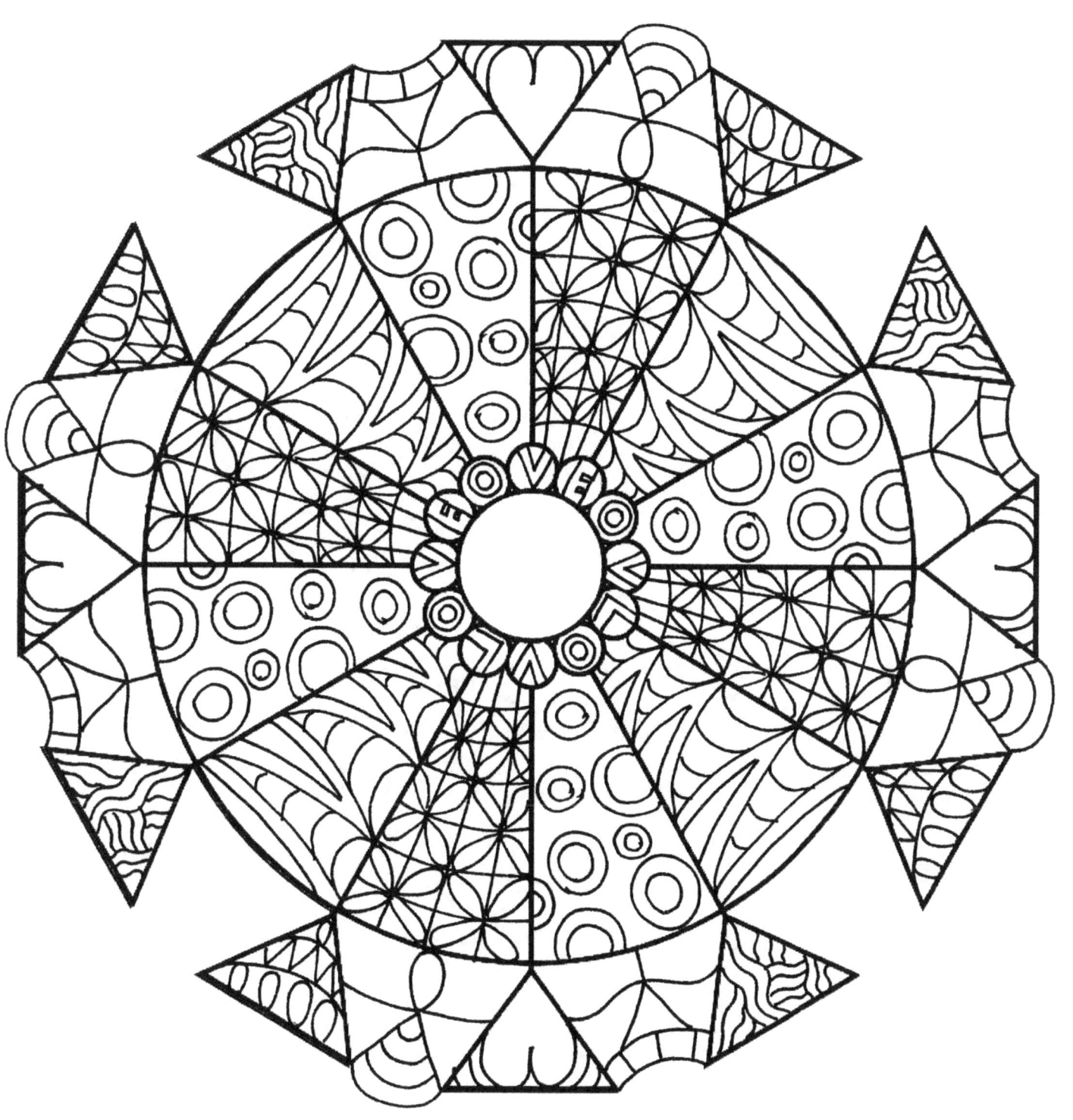

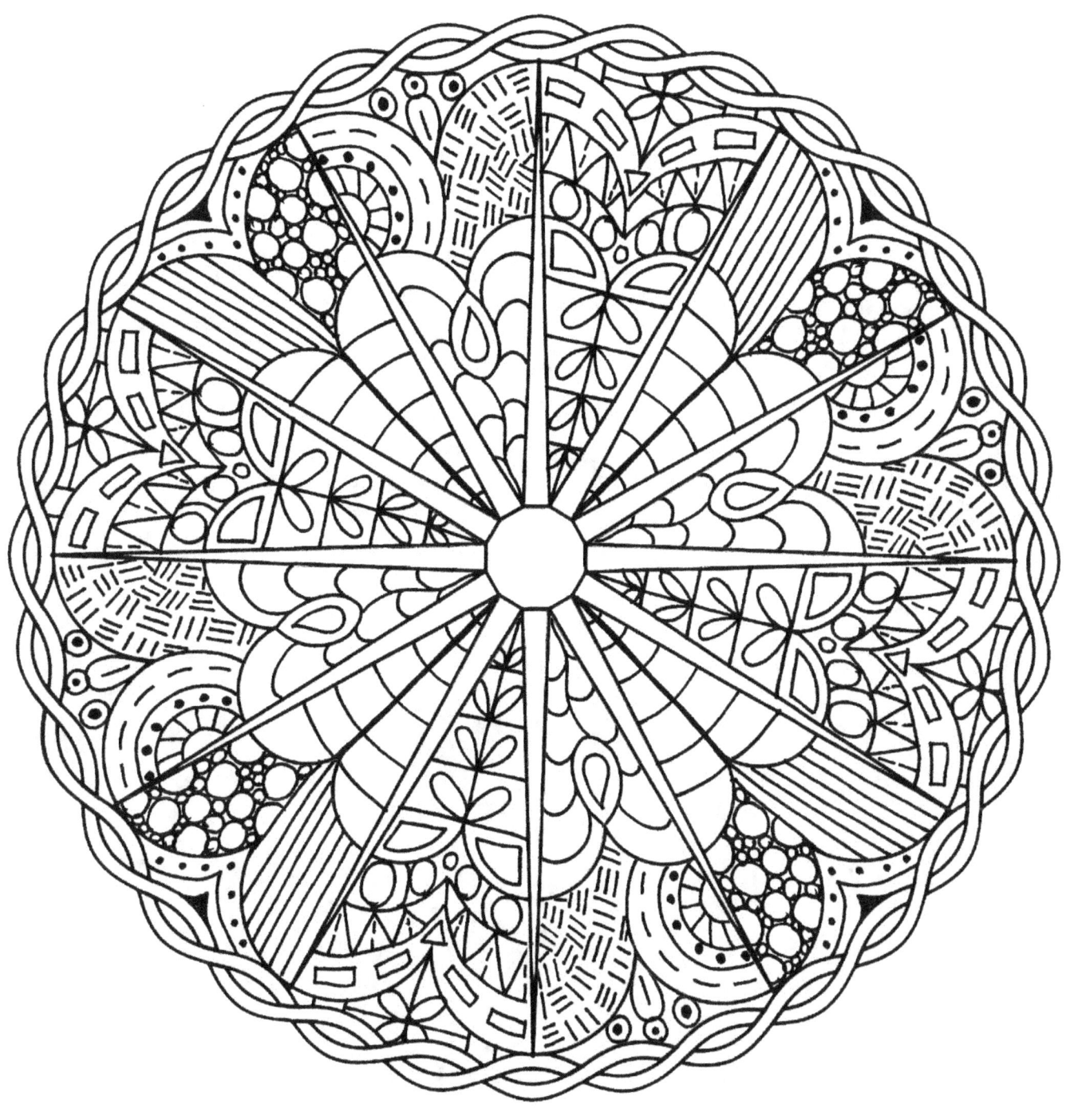

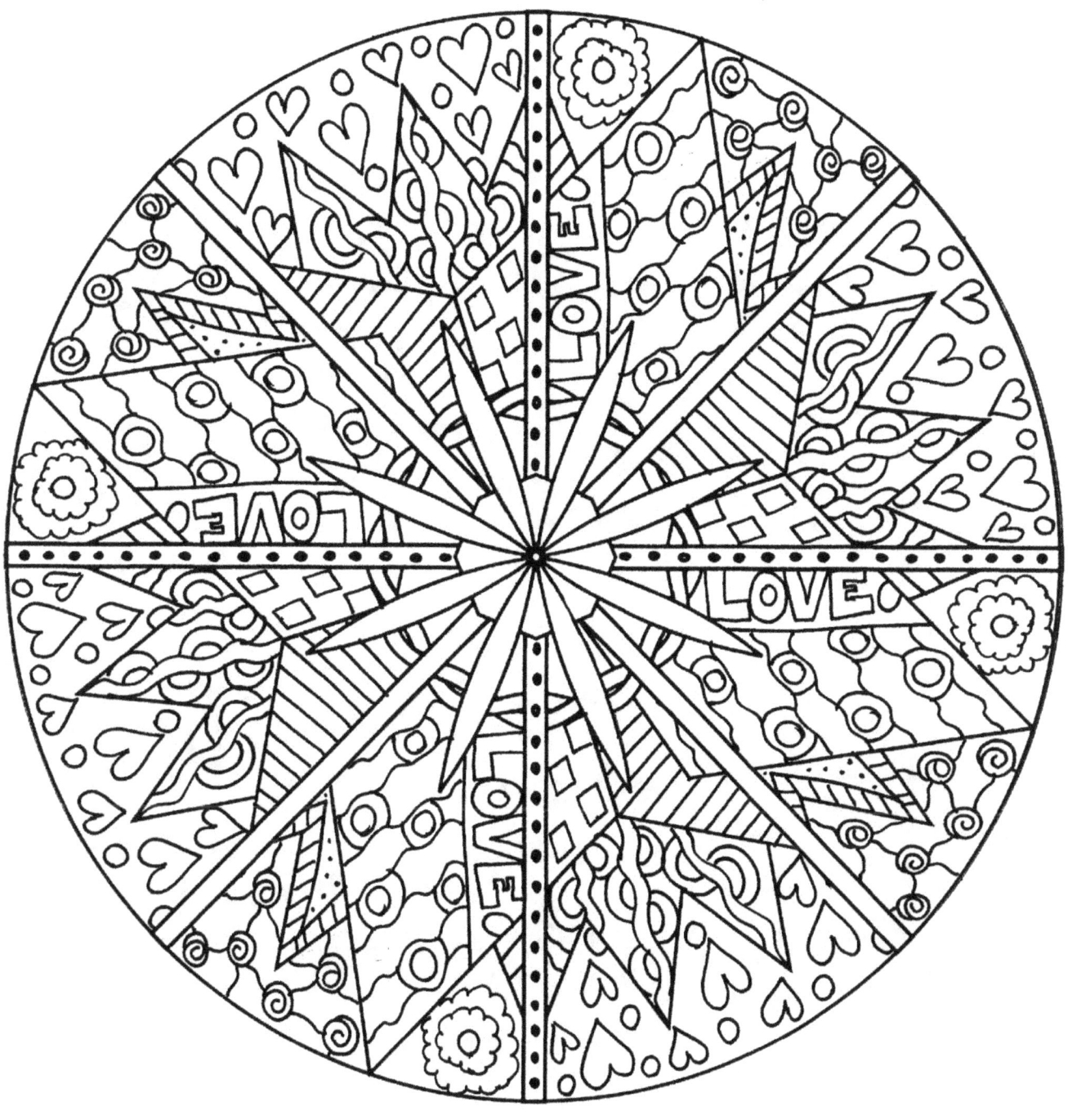

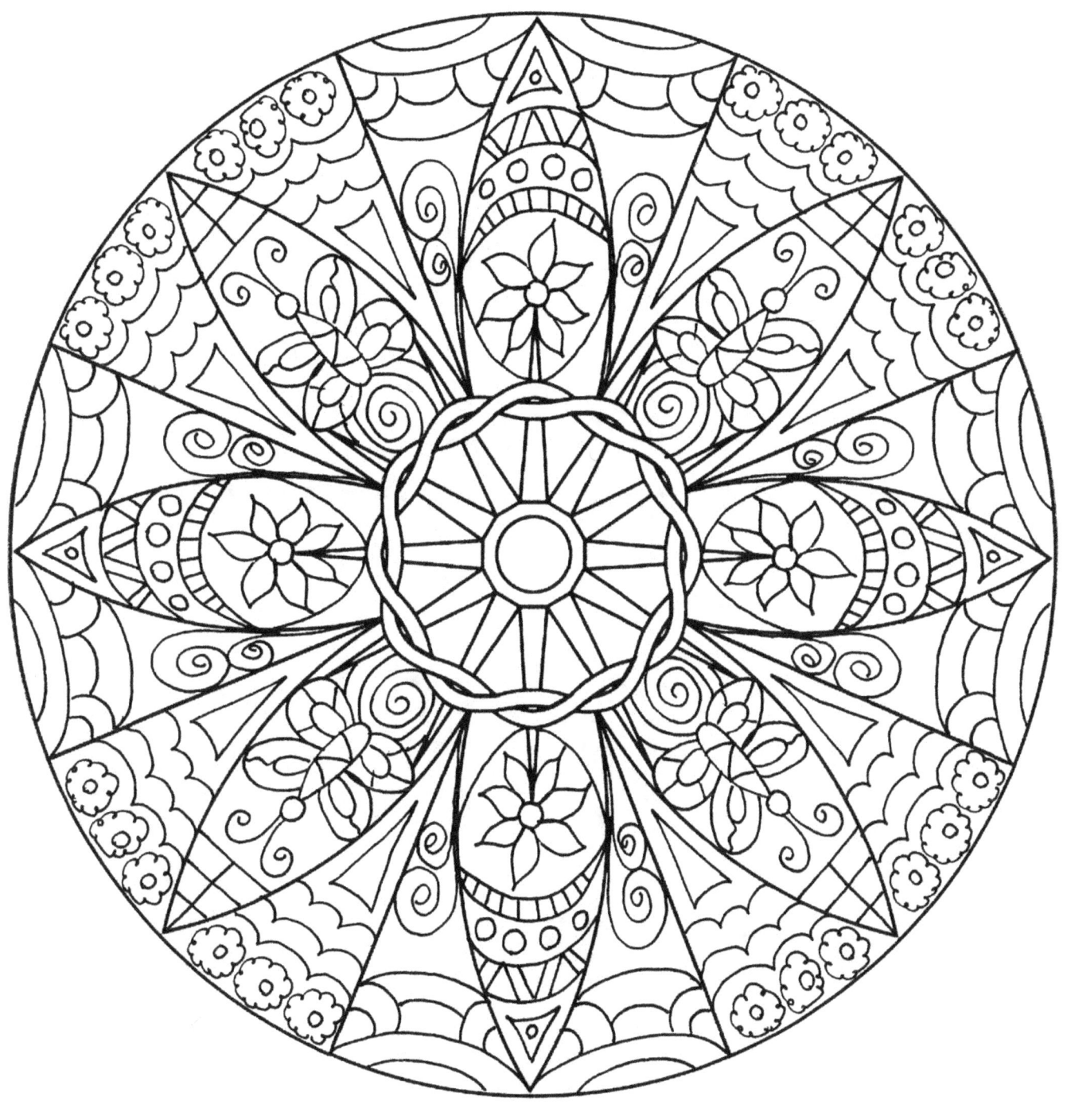

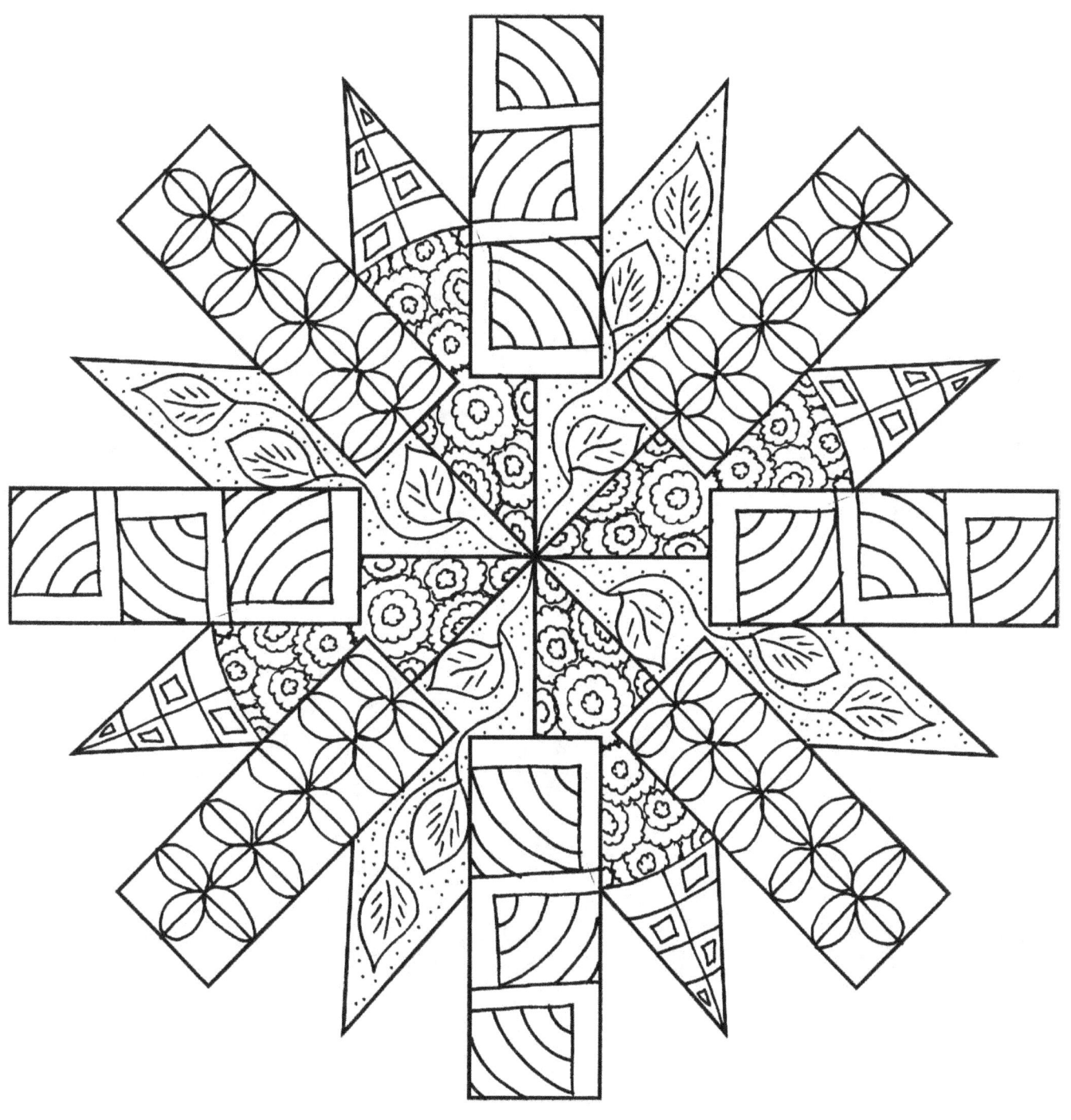

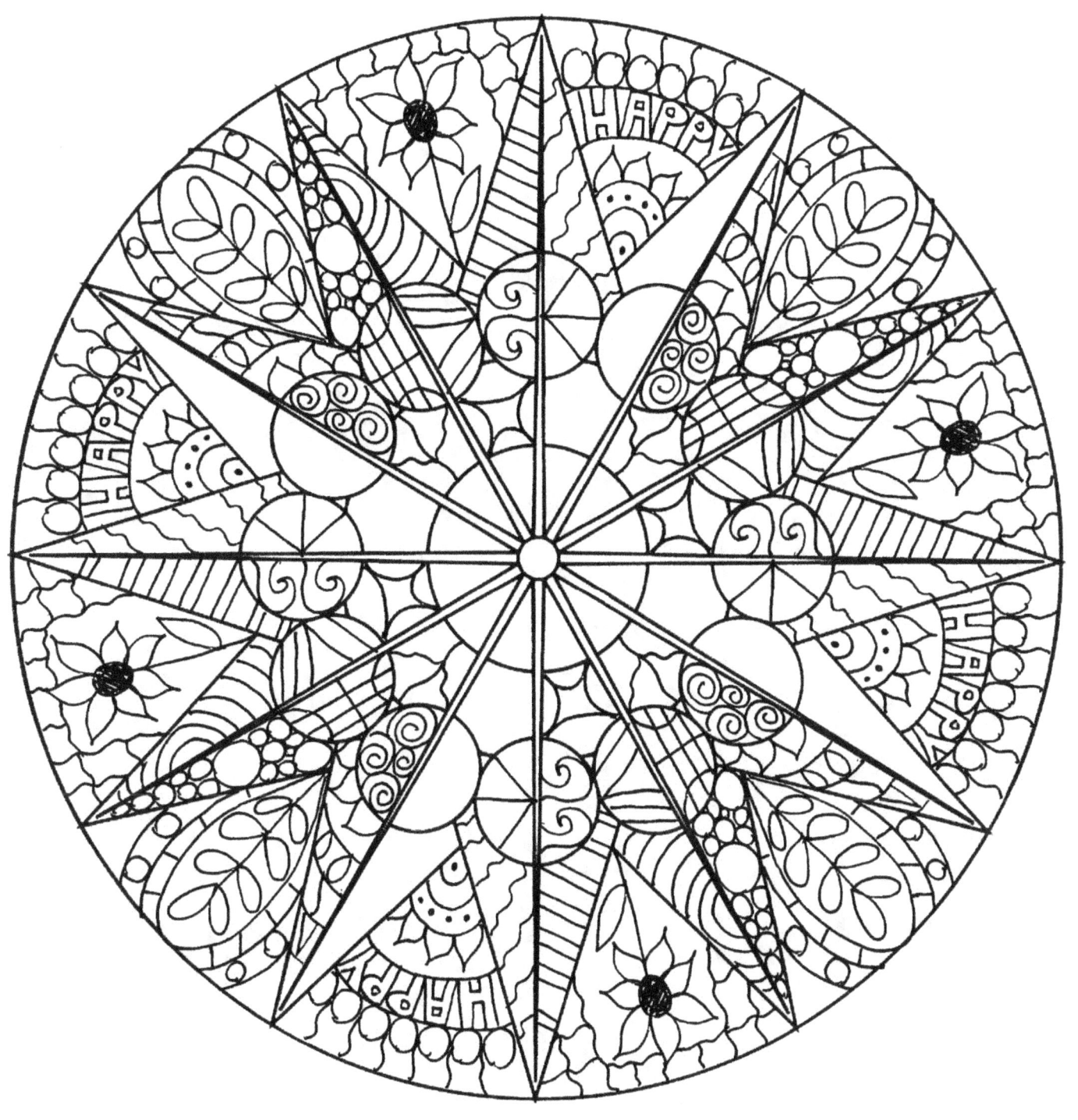

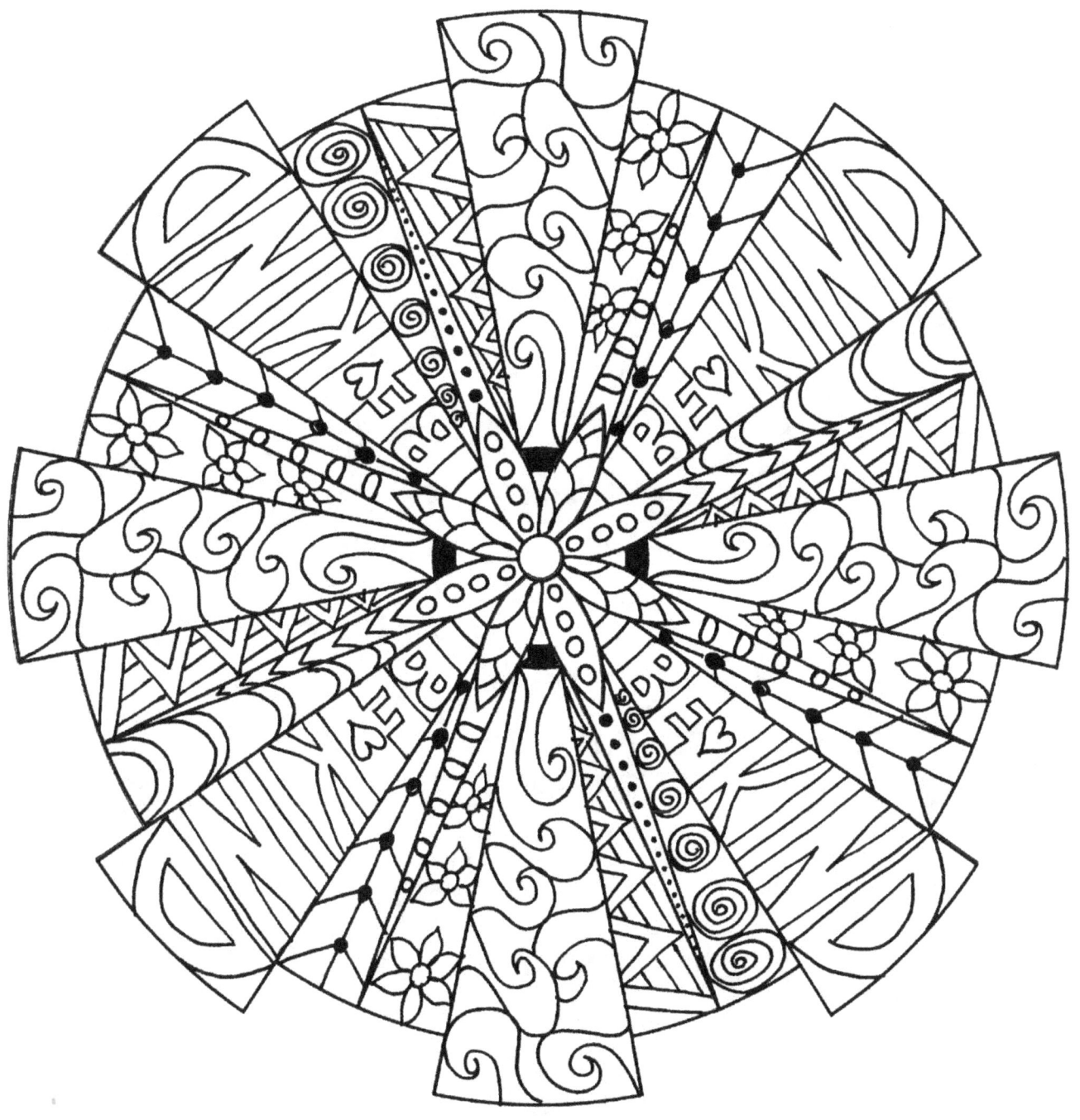

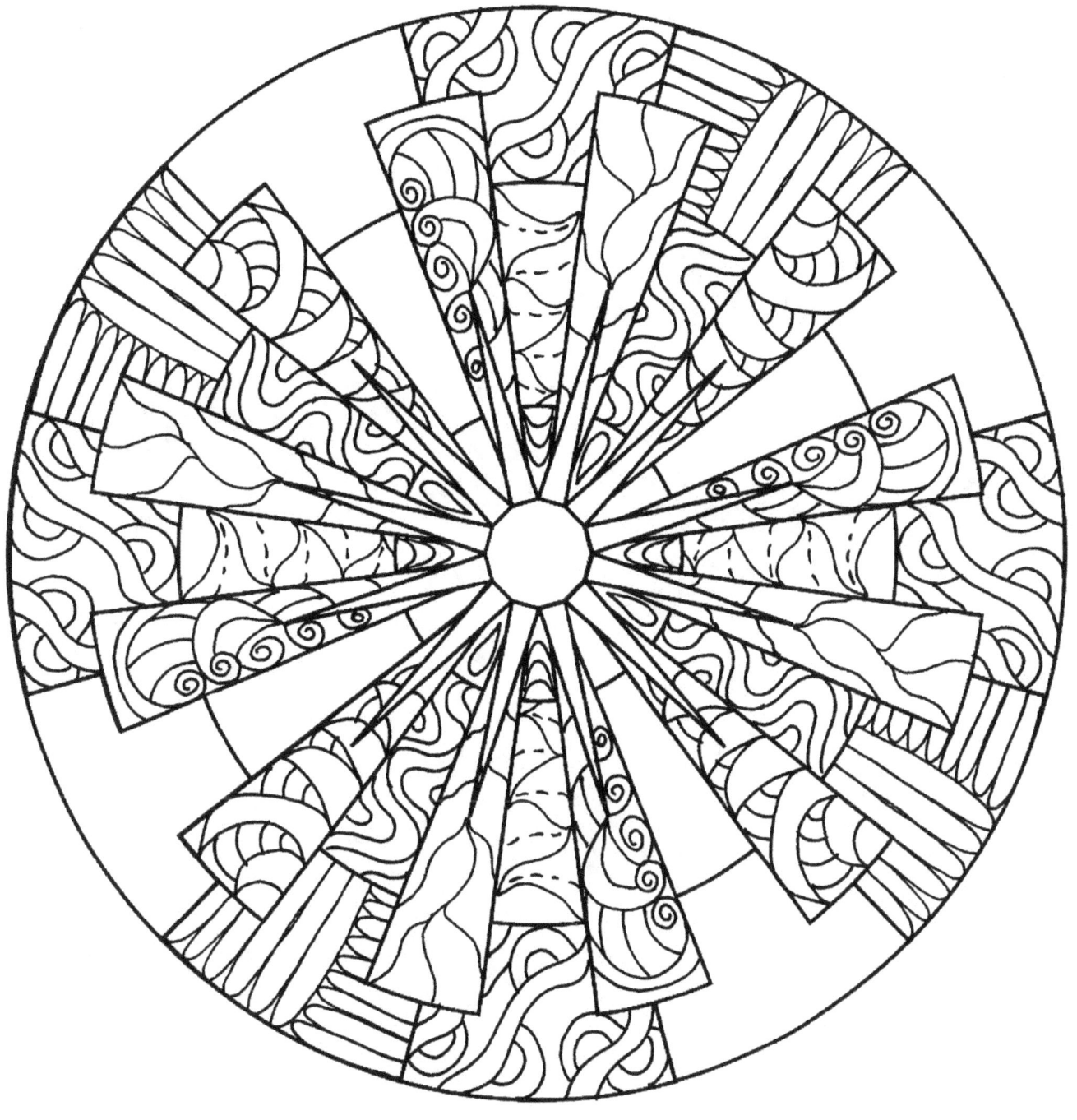

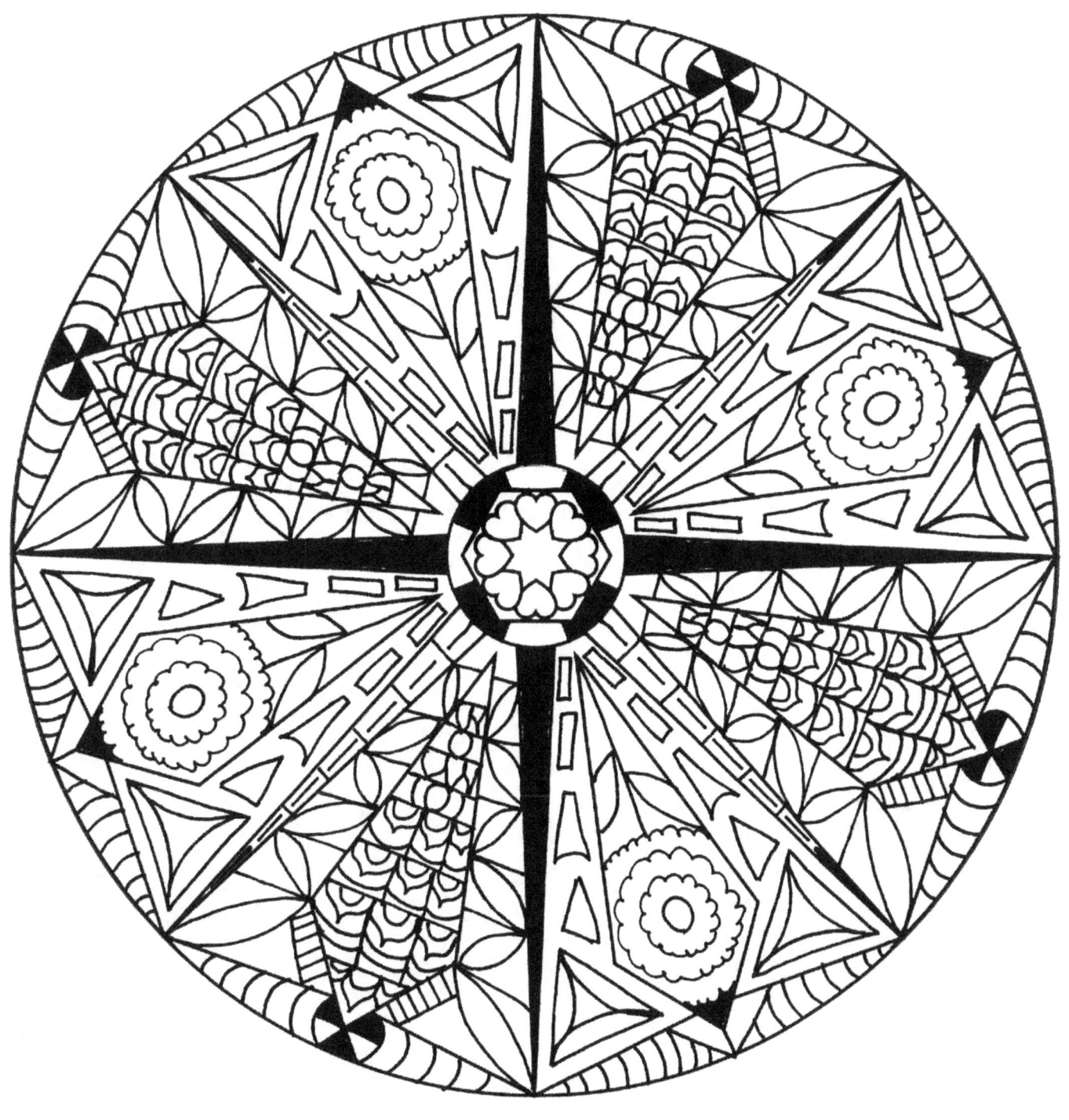

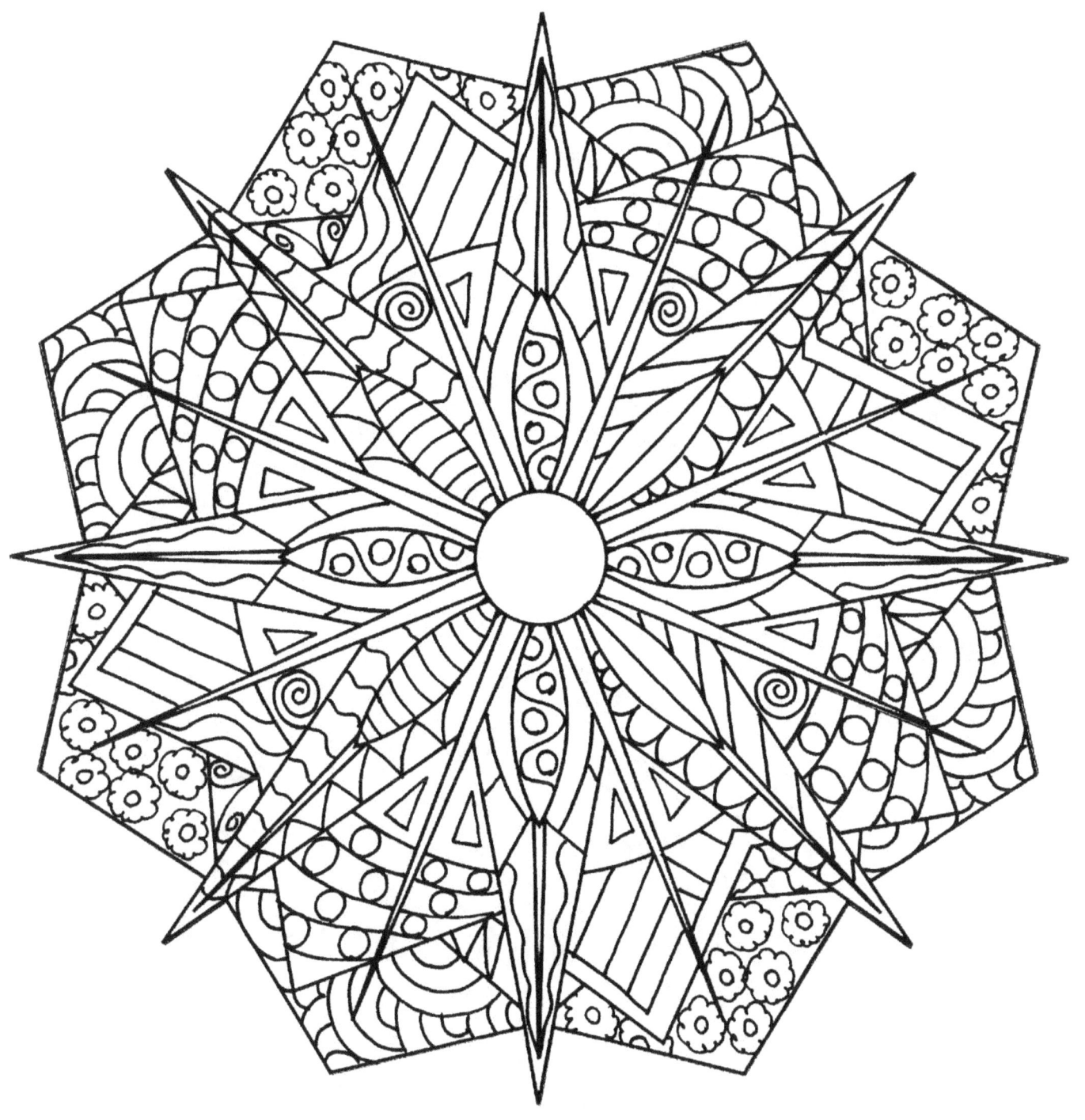

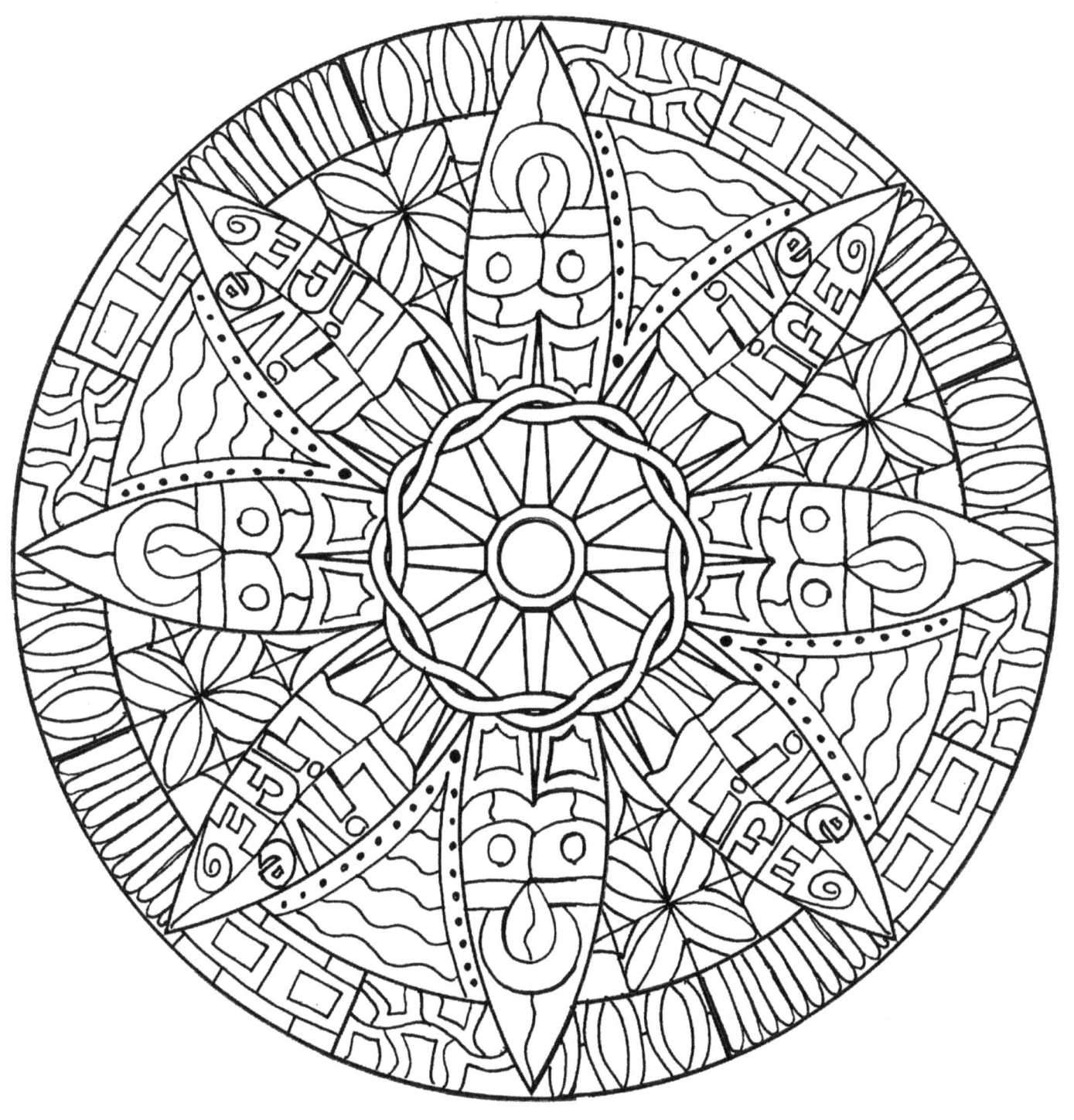

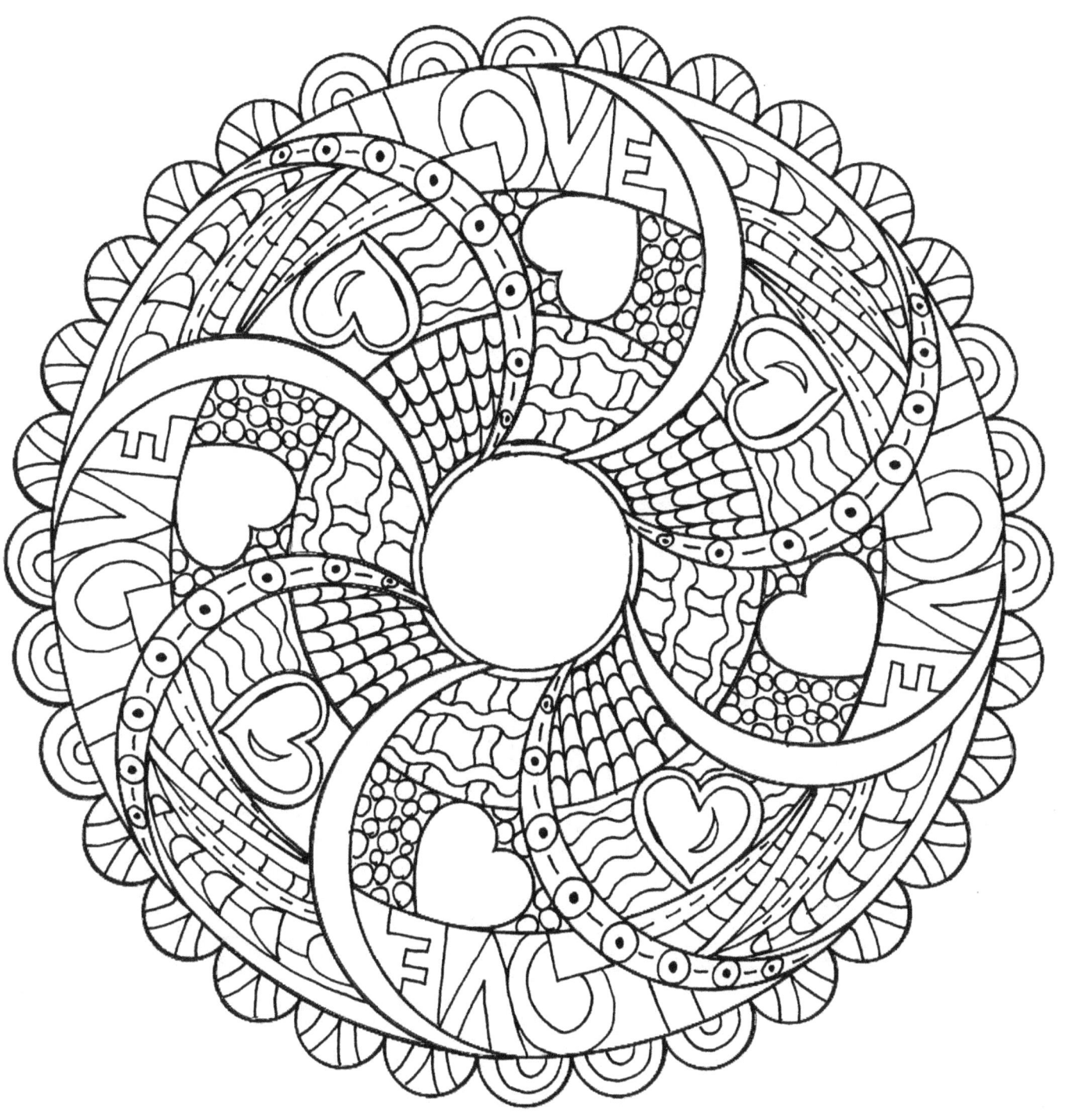

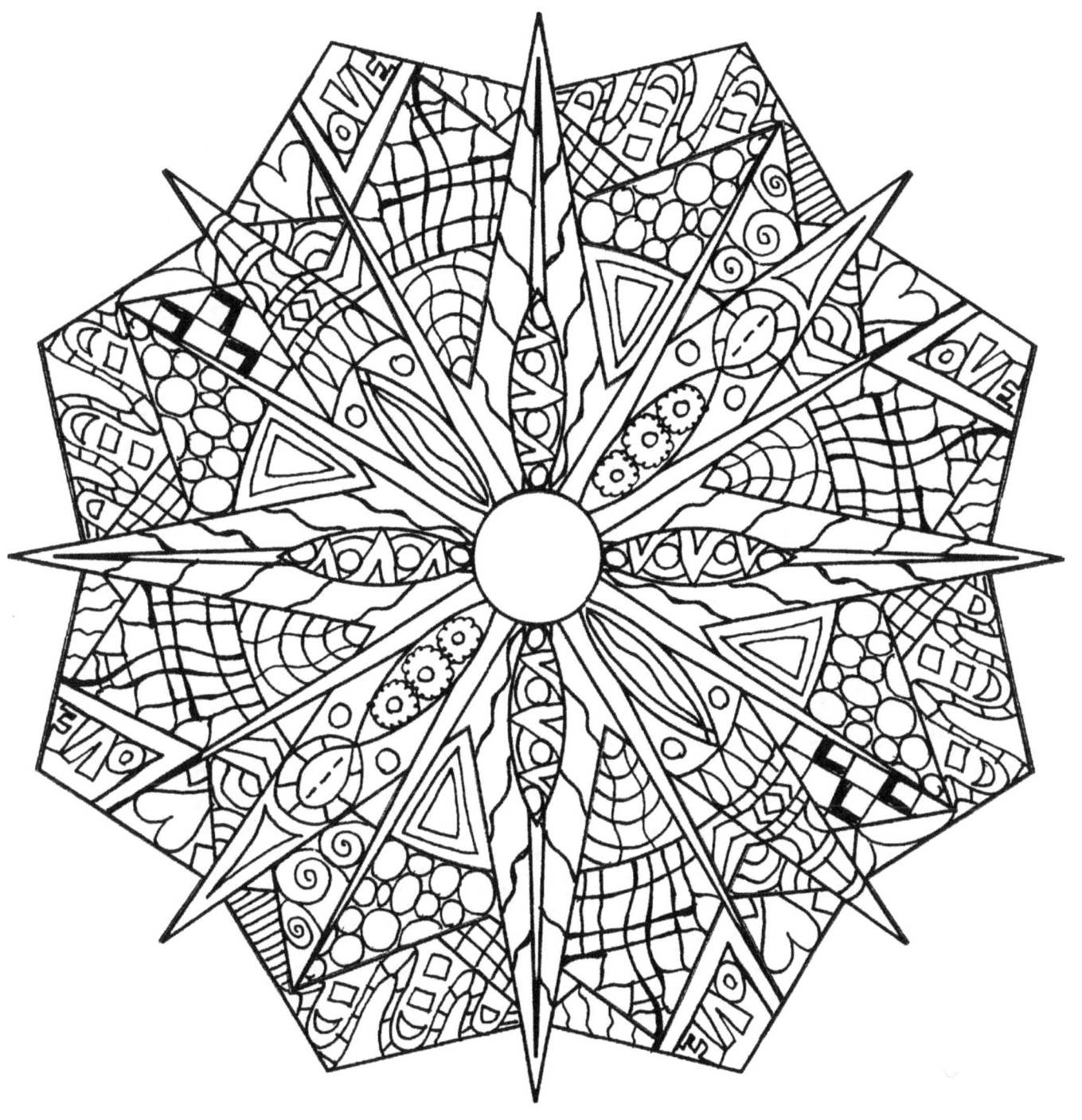

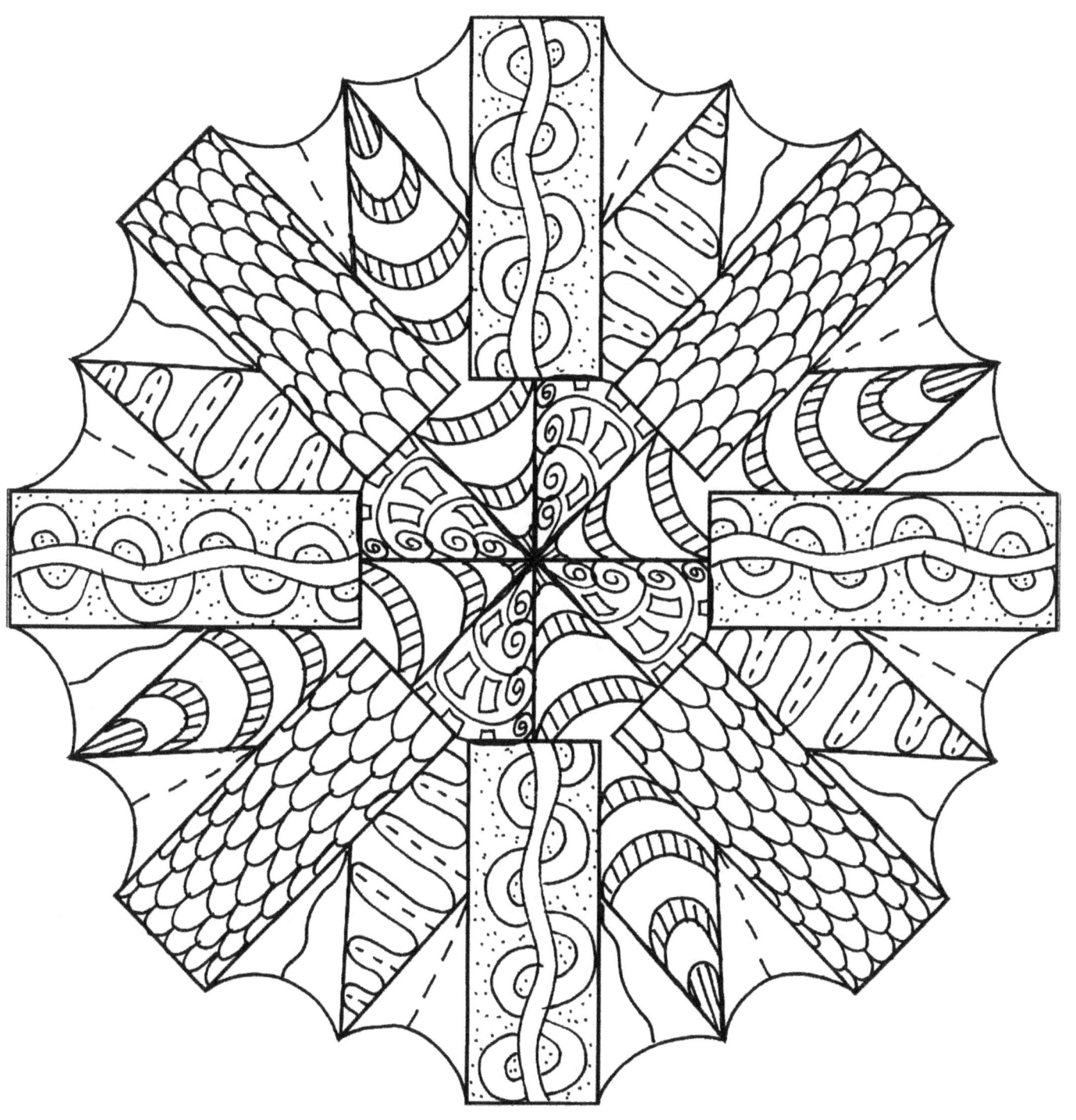

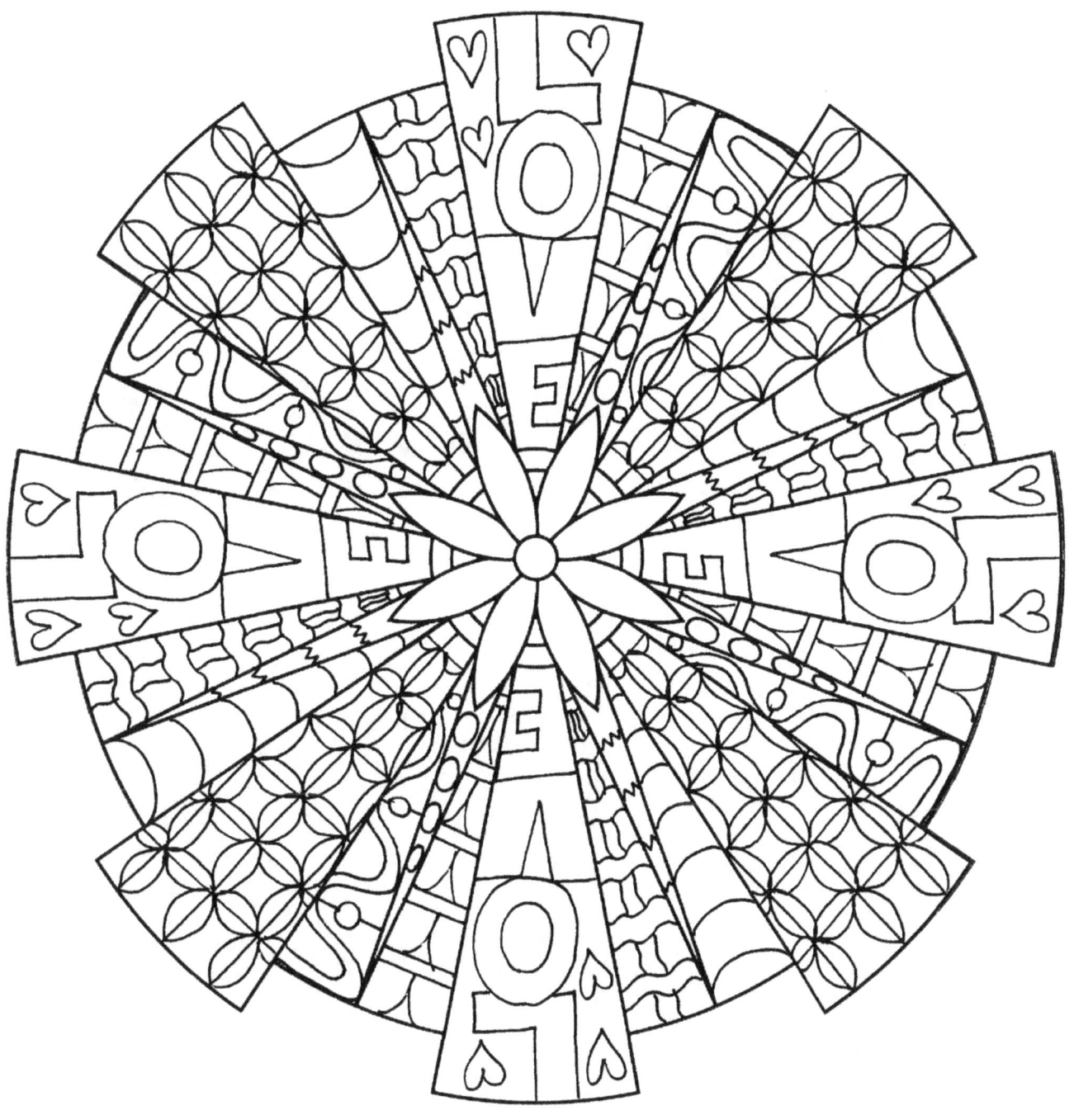

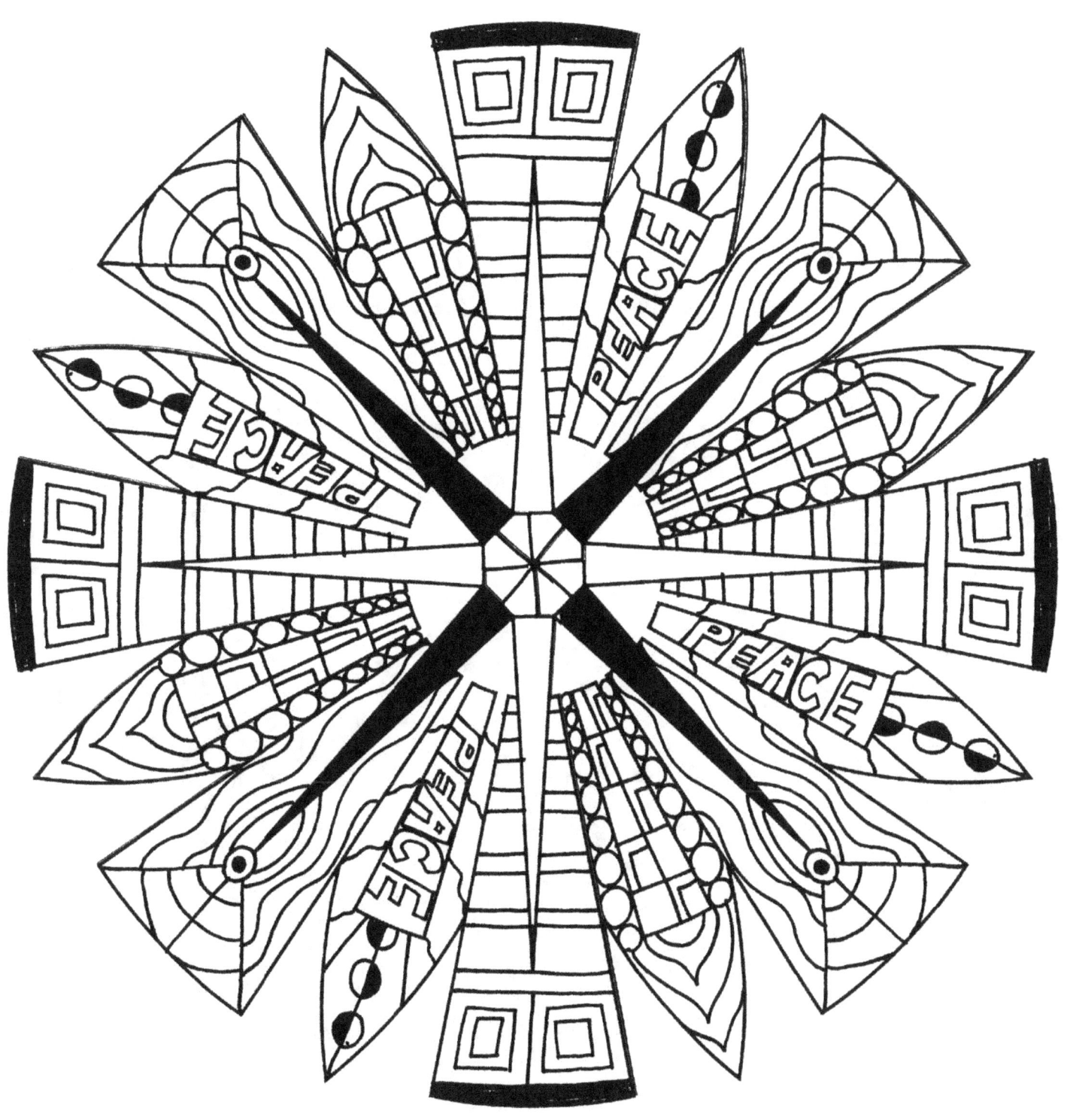

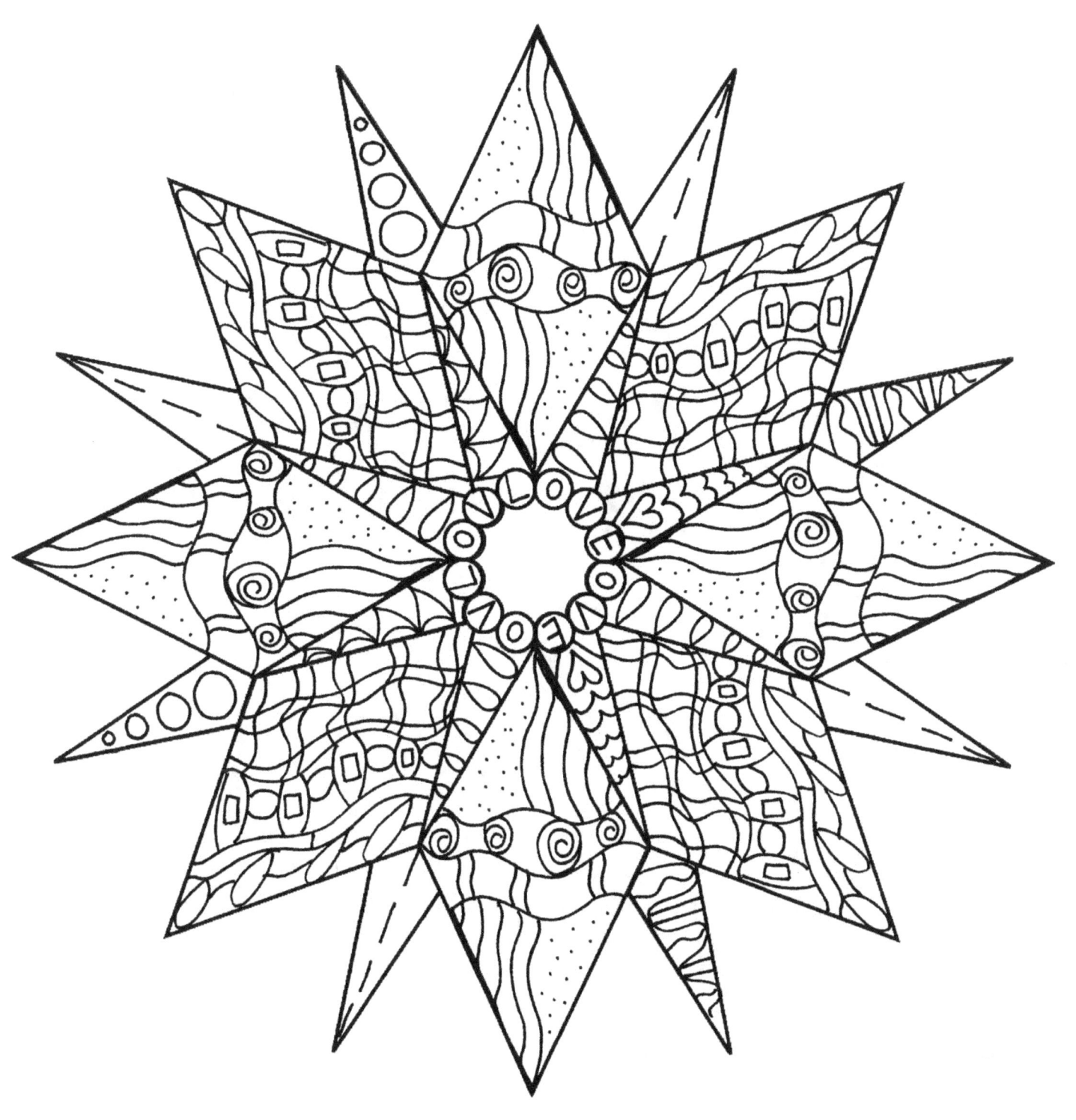

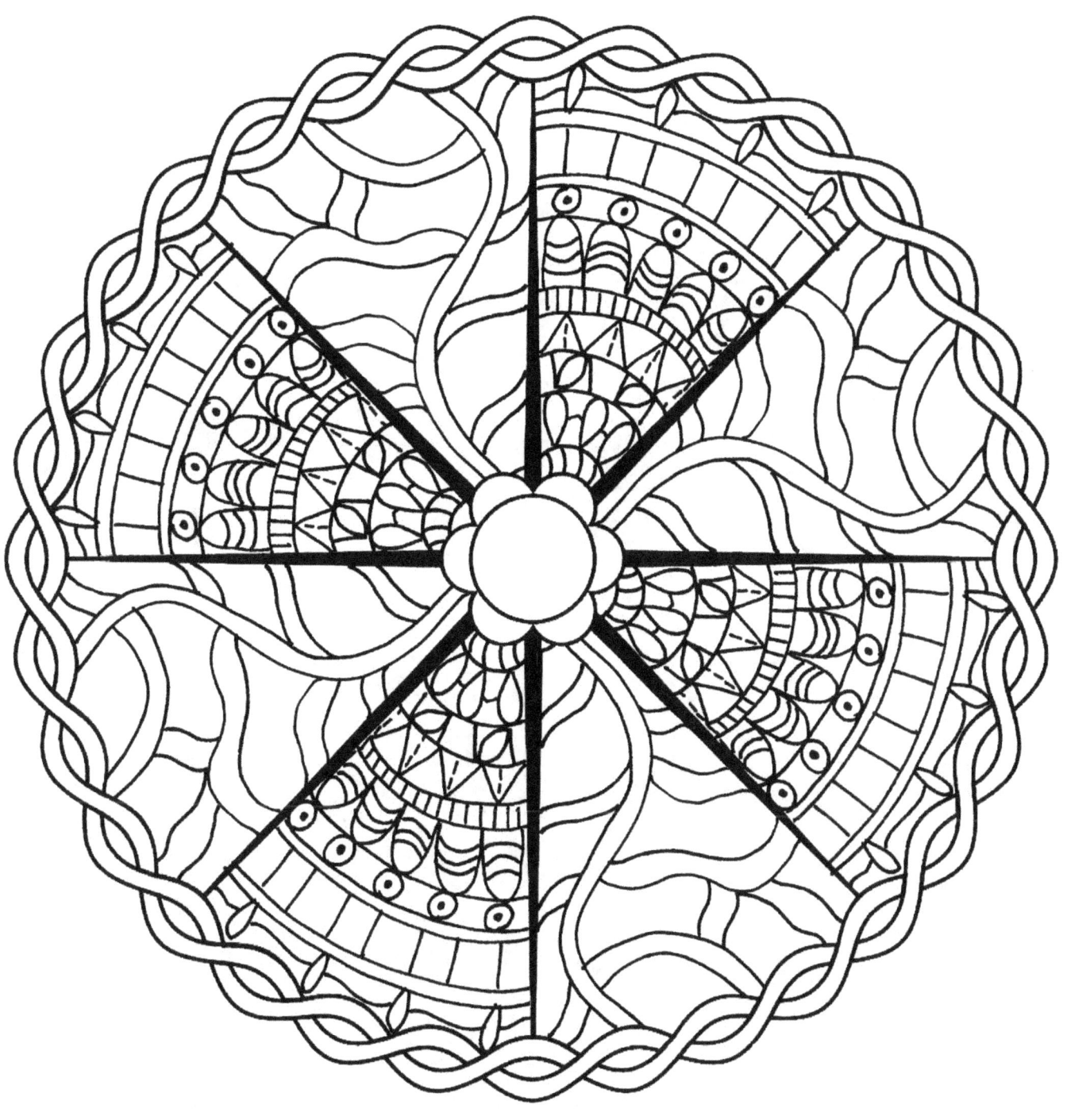

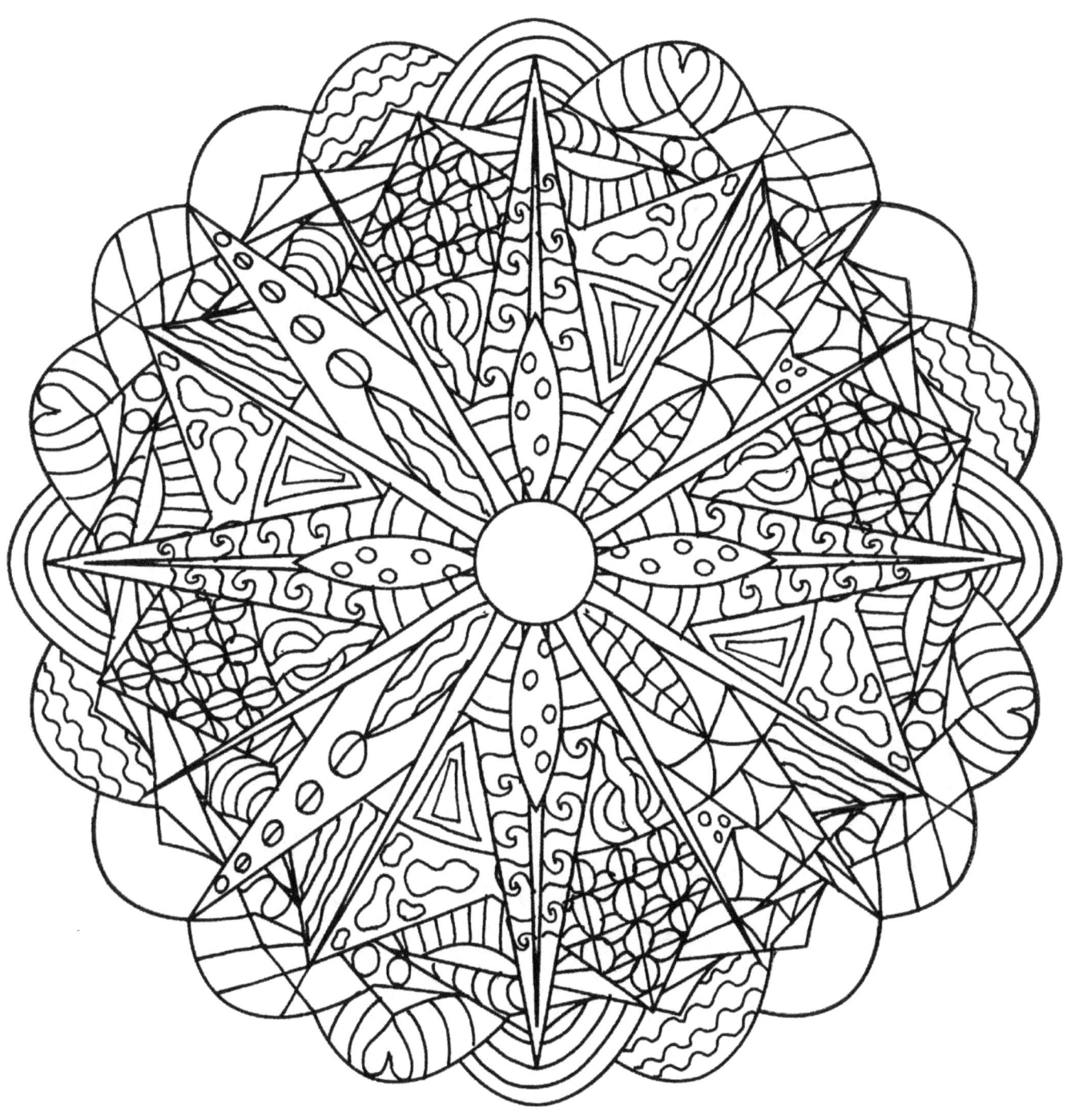

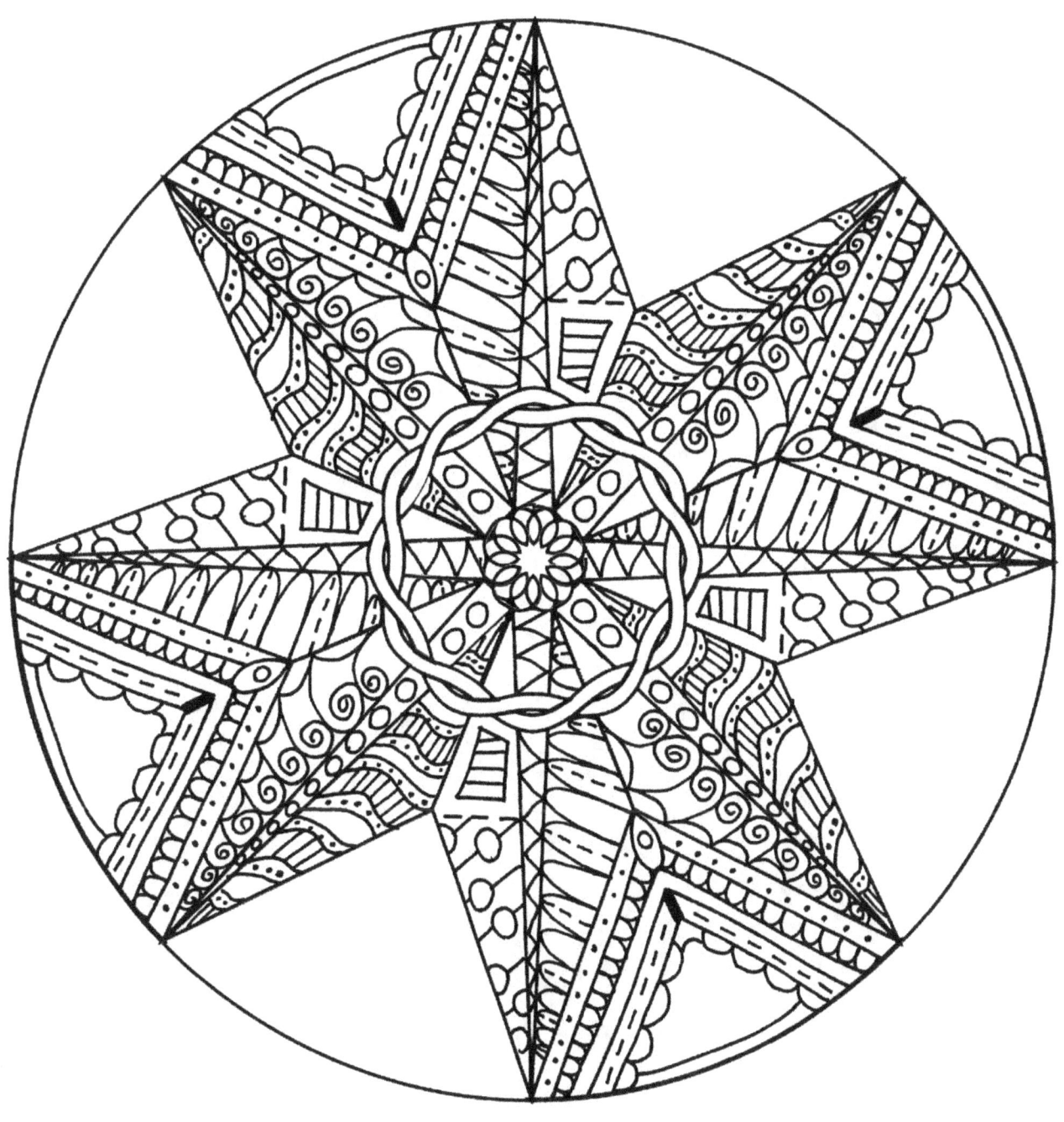

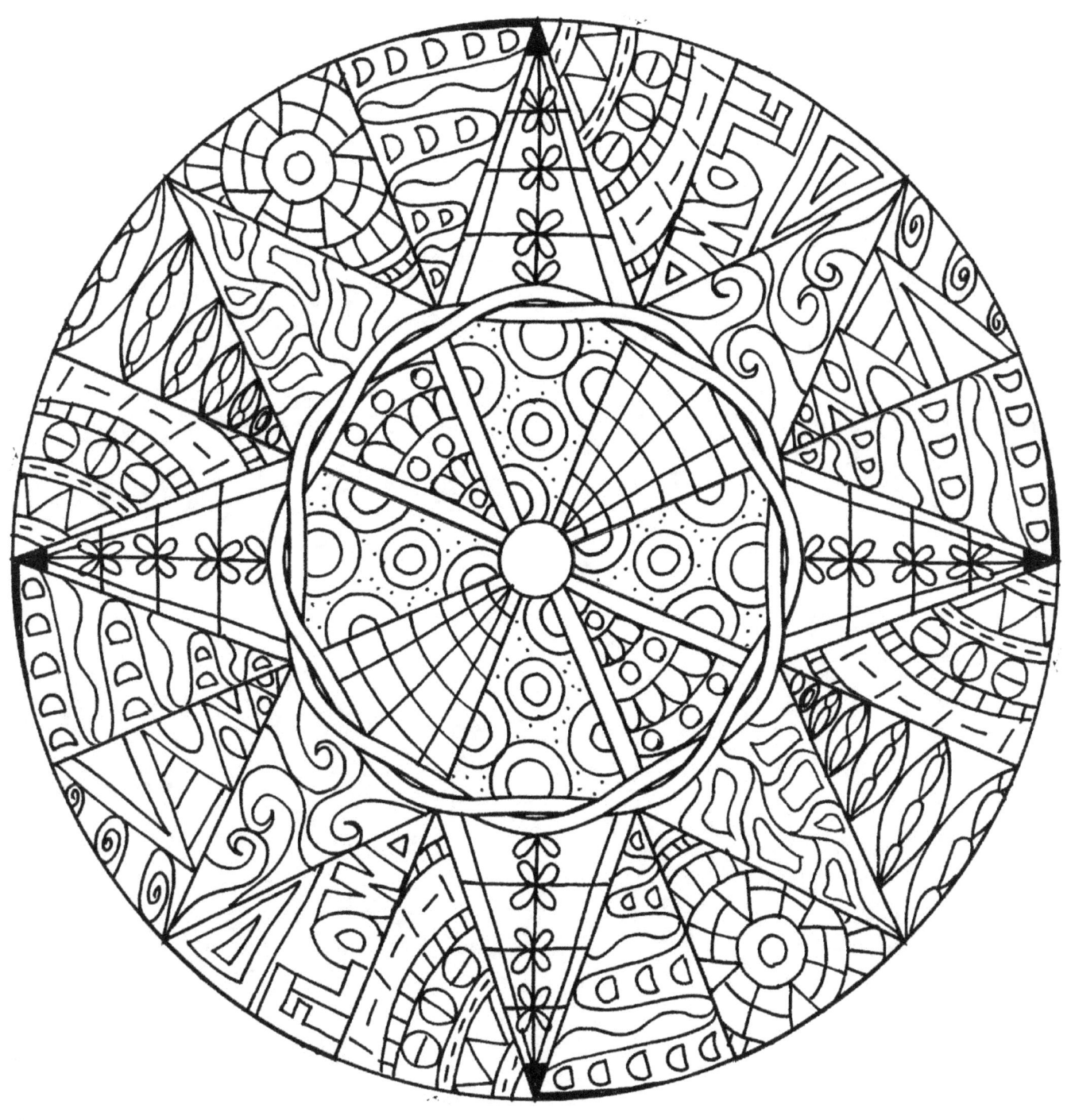

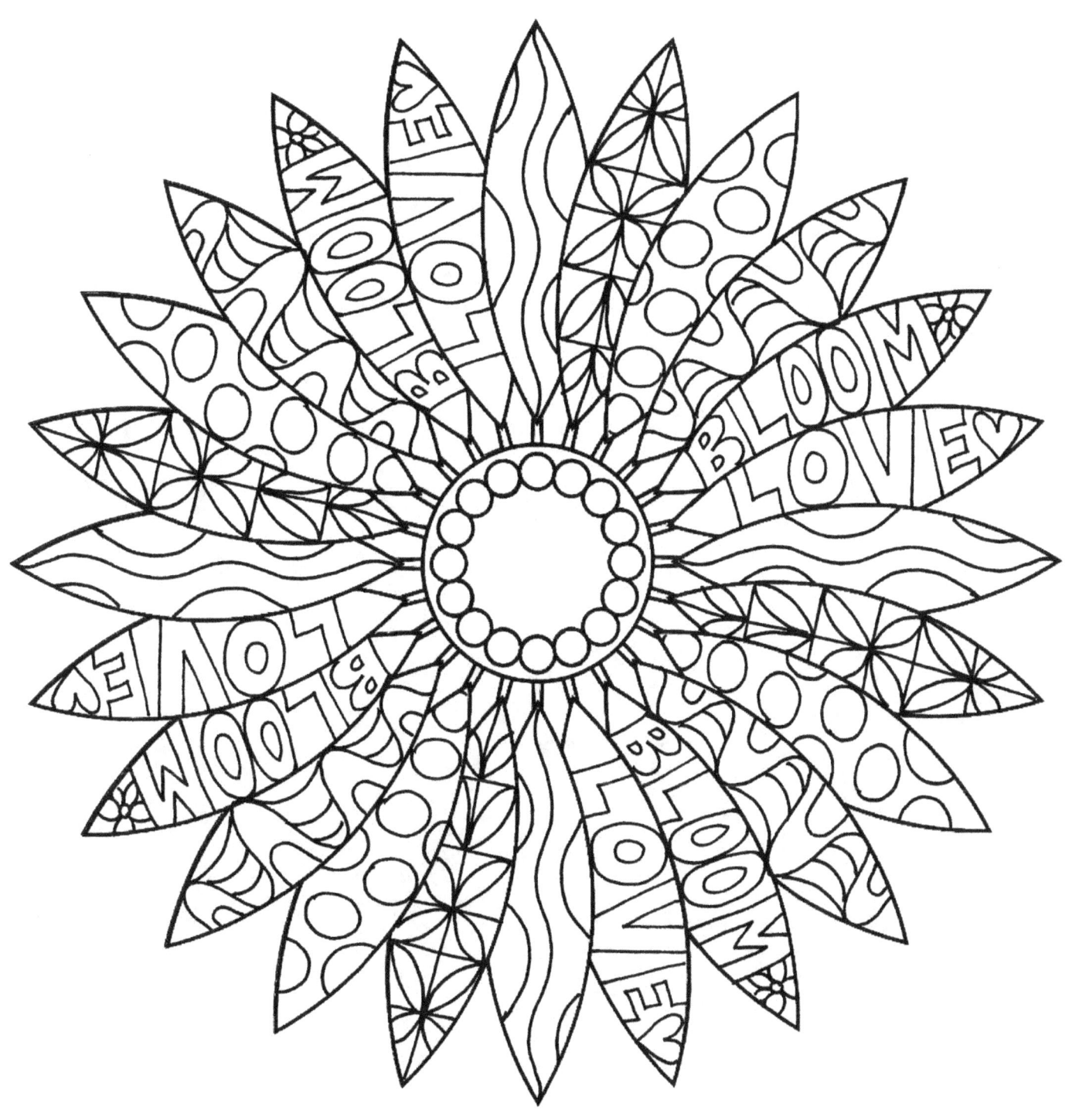

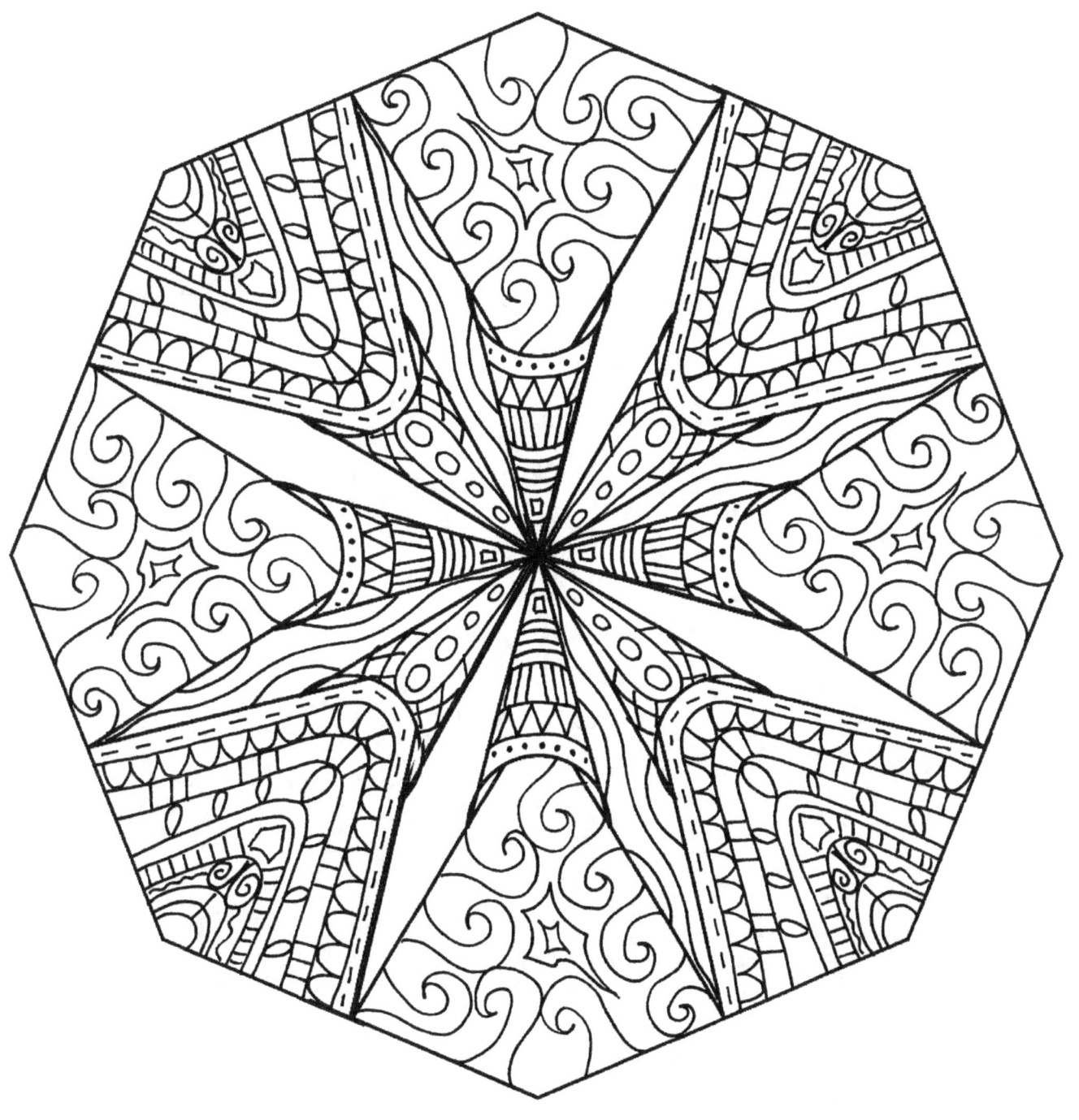

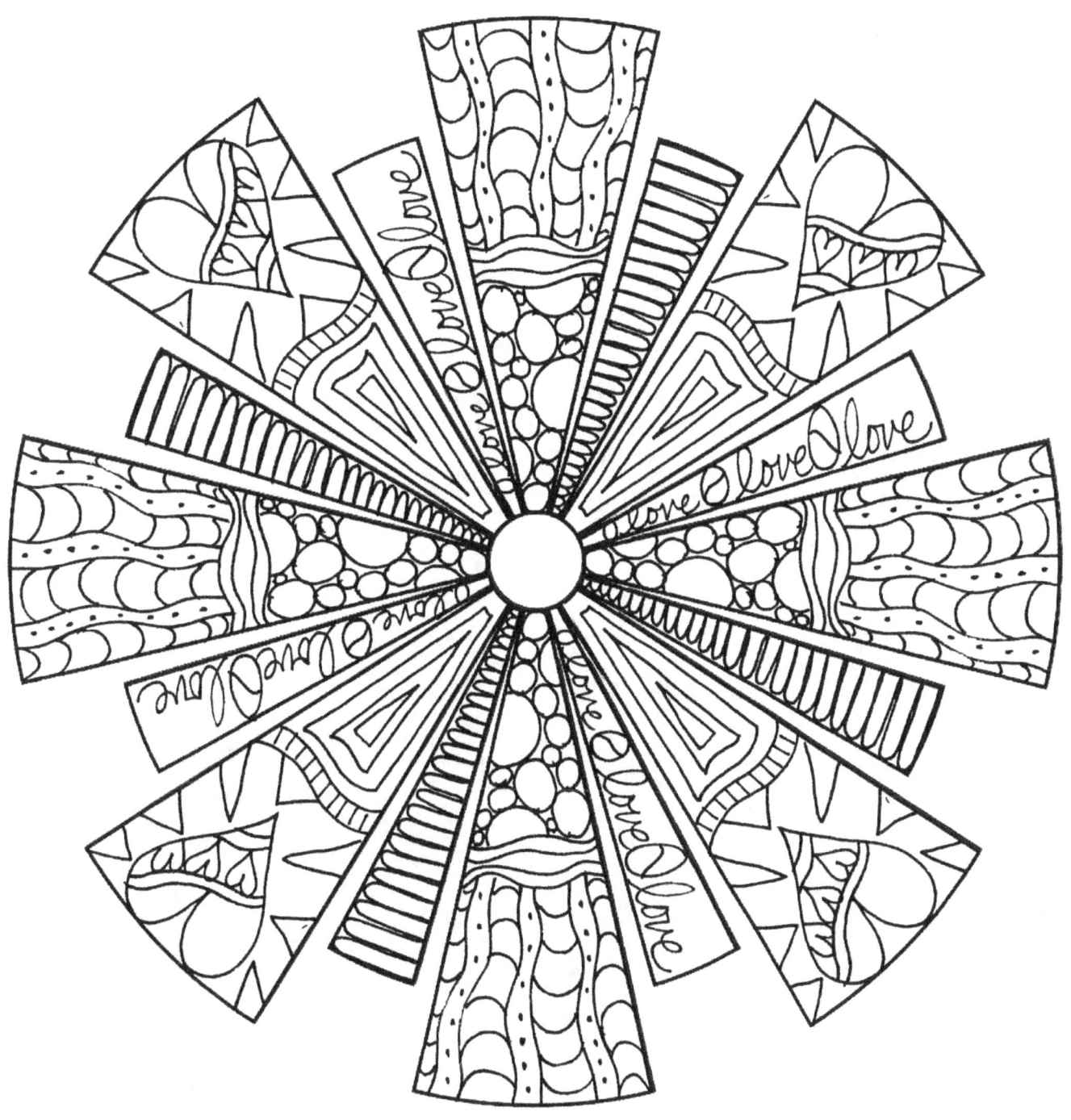

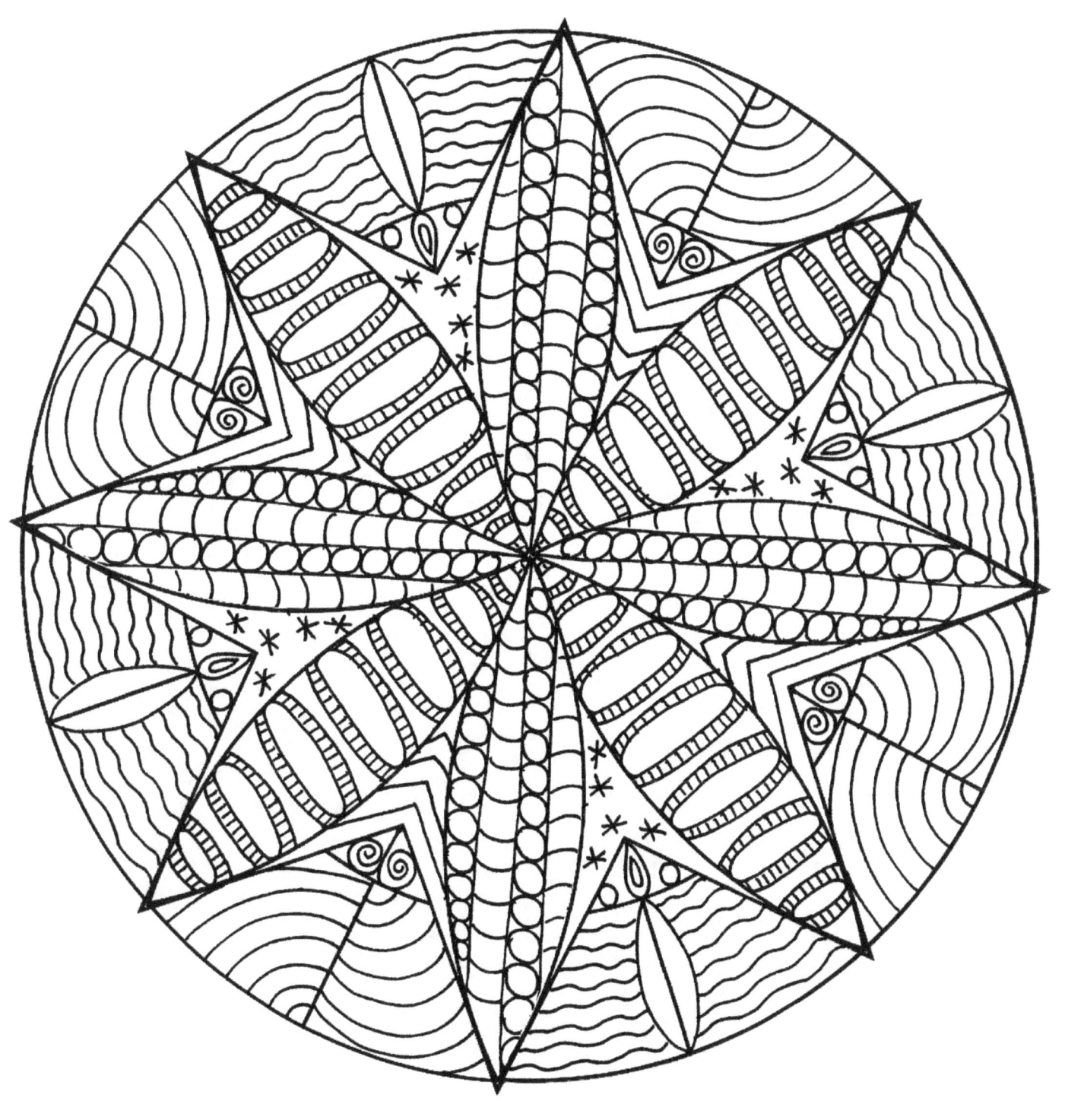

ABOUT THE ARTIST

Kim A. Flodin, whose artwork is marketed under the name Keleki Love, is also an intuitive energy healer who infuses each and every piece of her fun and flowing artwork with happy, healing, positive vibes.
When she's not busy creating art, you may find her hula hooping and chatting with the hummingbirds in the backyard. ☺

Learn more about her and her art, and see more art at: http://kelekilove.wix.com/kelekilove